PLOWED UNDER

A Young Girl's Obedience. God's Ever-Present Grace.

I0802014

PLOWED UNDER

A Young Girl's Obedience. God's Ever-Present Grace.

Amy Carmichael

(Originally published as
Ploughed Under: The Story of a Little Lover)

"O God, wert Thou ploughing
Thy profitless earth
With the brave plough of Love,
And the sharp plough of Pain?
But hark to the mirth
Of wheat-field in harvest! Dear Plougher, well worth
That ploughing, this yellow-gold grain."

Valley of Vision

A DOHNAVUR BOOK

CLC PUBLICATIONS
Fort Washington, PA 19034

Plowed Under
(Originally published as *Ploughed Under: The Story of a Little Lover*)

Published by CLC Publications

USA: P.O. Box 1449, Fort Washington, PA 19034
www.clcpublications.com

UK: Kingsway CLC Trust
Unit 5, Glendale Avenue, Sandycroft, Flintshire, CH5 2QP
www.equippingthechurch.com

First published 1934, London
First American edition 2013

This printing 2024

Printed in the United States of America

ISBN-13 (paperback): 978-1-61958-082-4
ISBN-13 (e-book): 978-1-61958-083-1

Italics in Scripture quotations are the emphasis of the author.

Notes on Words

Ammal, woman, lady; may be used of anyone from a beggar to a queen. (First *a* pronounced like *u* in *up*, second like *ah*.)

Amma, vocative of ammal. (Pronunciation as above.)

Amma, mother. (Pronunciation as above.)

Bandy, corruption of vandi, bullock-cart (*van* rhymes with *fun*).

Chee, word of utter opprobrium.

Clan, here used in the old Scottish sense of a family with a common ancestor, a family holding together, a coterie within a caste.

Iyer, a title of respect used for ordained men.

Taluk, a division of a district.

Tamasha, any sort of jubilation or celebration (second *a* pronounced like *ah*).

2nd person singular, used by older to younger and greater to less.

2nd person plural, an honorific. Often used in prayer by a new convert till the Christian usage becomes familiar.

Notes on Photographs

THE ripe corn, willow catkins, wild strawberries and fern are from that artist in photography, Herr Groh of Munich; the silver birch, the wintergreen, and the Christmas roses are from Dr. Defner of Innsbruck, friend of the little *Rose from Brier.*

The others were taken by one of our Fellowship, Frances Beath, when she and Star toured in the taluk of Vishnu's-heaven in 1933, and our old friends, the Vandyck Printers, have once more done their lovely work for us.

The photograph of the road to the temple of Great-Lake is to us a road leading out into the unknown and the unimagined, for it was from this temple the first little child was drawn as by an angel's hand. And so began that which was afterwards to be the Dohnavur Fellowship.

About the Story

THE child of this story, the little lover Arulai Tara, Star of Grace, had been ill. To relieve the tediousness of convalescence I gave her a bazaar notebook and a pencil, and said to her in effect, "Write what you can of the coming of the call of the unseen Spring."

For many crowded years the notebook lay overlooked. Then Star remembered it, and searched for it, meaning to destroy it. But I had retrieved it, and had found in its almost illegible pencil things too dear to forget.

Then some old notes of my own emerged. I had thought of them as devoured by white ants or swept away in some tidying raid. And there were fragments of the same story in a book long out of print; and other fragments were scattered about the green field of memory, like the broken loaves on the grass—"there was much grass in the place"—and there for a while they lay.

At last familiar words took shape: "Gather up the fragments that remain, that nothing be lost." And so they were gathered. But the story would never have been made into a book if it had not been for the Lotus Bud who typed it (it had to be written in pencil, just as Star's was) and for the Fellowship who wanted it; they helped in ways too many to tell.

The beautiful little *Book of the Lover and the Beloved* [1] helped too for this reason: "Ramon Lull is never unmindful of the world his Beloved came to save. His is no cloistered love. He could never say, with St. John of the Cross, 'Live in the world as though there were in it but God and thy soul.' Ringing for ever in his ears is the Beloved's last command." And *Plowed Under* is the story of the preparation of a little lover for obedience to that command.

Whoso loveth knoweth the sound of this voice.

A.C.

Dohnavur, Tinnevelly, South India.

Contents

List of Illustrations

YET again the soul breaks away to its own, with the natural flight of a bird from its Autumn nest at the call of an unseen Spring, to the far-off land that is nearer still than its nest, because it is in its heart.

From the Introduction to *Revelations of Divine Love*, recorded by Julian, Anchoress of Norwich, edited by Grace Warrack.

Come ill, or well, the cross, the crown,
The rainbow or the thunder—
I fling my soul and body down
For God to plough them under.

Songs of Travel, R.L.S.

1

The Call of the Spring

IN the early evening, when the hills in the distance showed faint and blue, in a patch of rough ground called Field of the Darling-Pool a little girl stood alone. She was barely ten, but for what seemed to her a long time she had been asking questions which no one could answer, not even her wise old father to whom she had shyly brought them.

There was something austere about the child, something that, in the mood which was upon her then, would have made one who saw her think of a little grey rock cropping up among greenery. But there was something wistful too. She was wrapped in a sari, bright like a blackberry leaf in September, or the breast of a forest minivet, the one warm note of color there, and she waited, still as a leaf, for something to happen, for someone to speak.

The place known by that affectionate name (because of a spring, which in the Rains became a large pool) was near the prosperous country town of Uncrowned-King in the taluk called Vishnu's-heaven. The child, whose home was there, waited patiently. There was no one anywhere in sight.

Who of all the gods was the God of gods, the Sovereign God, Creator? That had been the first question that she had brought to her father. Was it the heavenly Siva, whose ashes she rubbed on her forehead every morning after bathing? There were so many gods, she grew puzzled as she counted them all. Who was the greatest? *Was* it Siva? Could he change dispositions? If only she could find this out she would be satisfied, for the god who could change dispositions must be the greatest, and surely the greatest must be Creator. Her father had not seemed to know of any god who could do that kind of thing. Gods were to be feared and worshipped. They caused or averted disaster. They did not concern themselves with the dispositions of children. And he had tried to put her off. This had disheartened her, but she had not given up hope of discovering Him whom she sought. There was one way, she reflected, by which she could bring creatorship and sovereignty down to the test of practical life. She would go through all the gods she knew and find out which of them could change dispositions. She decided to begin with Siva, whose name her clansmen bore. Had not her father gone to his temple month by month, with fasting and with prayer, praying for children to be born to him? And had not the heavenly Siva granted him eleven (of whom she was the fifth, and a certain little girl known now to many as Mimosa, the sixth)? Her heart went out to Siva with trustful expectation. *He* would change her disposition.

For she had a hot temper. Often when she was playing with other children (always excepting a boy cousin a few years older than herself), something would provoke her, and she would break out in anger, whereupon they would run away and refuse to play with her. She had tried to conquer the fault, but there it was, strong, and growing stronger in her. She prayed to Siva, crying over and over into the air that never answered her back again, "O heavenly Siva, hear me! Change my disposition so that other children may love me and wish to play with me. O heavenly Siva, hear me! hear me!"

But her disposition had not been changed. She had appealed to several other gods, but nothing had happened. And now again the longing for knowledge, for deliverance, for One whom she could adore, to whom she could pour out the love of her heart, was upon her, and she had come to the field where no one could see her. She was all alone now—with whom?

She waited awhile in silence, the unanswering green things about her, the empty blue sky above her; she lay down with her forehead on the ground, prostrating herself as she had seen her elders do before the god in the temple, and she stretched out her arms and cried, "O God, God of all the gods, hear me!"

In one of T.E. Brown's poems he tells us that he "was in heaven one day when all the prayers came in," and he watched them being "sorted."

> Then did I see how the great sorter chose
> One flower that seemed to me a hedgeling rose,
>   And from the tangled press
>   Of that irregular loveliness
> Set it apart—and, "This," I heard him say,
> "Is for the Master": so upon his way
> He would have passed; then I to him:—
> Whence is this rose, O thou of cherubim
> The chiefest?"—"Know'st thou not?" he said,
>   and smiled,
> *"This is the first prayer of a little child."*

All who have heard a child's first prayer or the first prayer of an older soul, but still a child in the new life, know why and with what expectant love that angel smiled.

But the child on her face on the ground did not see the angel smile; she did not see anything or hear anything. She rose, shook the dust from her sari, and ran home. And she tried to forget. But a passionate despair possessed her heart, a pain of desire that she could not understand. It had to be so. For when the Beloved discerns a lover in a soul, He fills that soul with consuming thirst, a thirst that no waters of earth can satisfy. It is then the call of the Spring is heard, that unseen Spring that draws the bird from the nest that once was home.

2

The Little Sanctuaries

HOME, to that child of the minivet-colored sari, meant a big white house, full of children, of whom the youngest, a beautiful boy called after one of the household gods, was her great delight. He was so winning that people passing down the street would turn to look at him; for he was "fair," as the word is used here (it means that the velvety skin of a child is in color like sunburnt ivory), and his brown eyes smiled at everyone. He was not troubled with smothering clothes. A silver belt made of bells that tinkled with every movement, gold and silver bangles on the little wrists and ankles—that was enough for him. He was his sister's nursling, for, young as she was herself, she had cared for him from the first hour of his life.

When he was nine months old, in the dreary wet weather, he died of a lingering dysentery. When his little body was carried away he left desolation behind him, especially in his sister's heart. Her mother tried to comfort her. She said that she had not wanted him to live because of the sin of the world; the eldest son of that family whose loving pride had named him after the family deity, the ancient god of Korkai, their ancestral city, was already its anxiety, and thinking of him the mother had sorrowfully prayed, "Let not my baby live to grow up." But the sad little sister was not comforted. She could not imagine anything so merry and so loving growing up hard and bad. Surely so sweet a thing would have been good? And now where was he? Where was that far away, that forlorn land of the spirits of the dead? He would be lonely, poor little cherished boy, among all those stranger spirits. No, there was no comfort anywhere, for no one could tell her anything comforting. So she found her way to a tamarind tree that grew near the Darling-Pool, and stood under its spreading branches, sick with misery and longing.

She had by this time almost given up hope of finding a God who could change dispositions; indeed, she had almost forgotten her quest in her absorbing grief, but she felt her way to a new and poignant question now. A Maker of such lovely things as a baby brother must be a great God, but was He good? Was it like a good God to give her such a little brother and then suddenly take him away? Would a good God disappoint, and hurt, and strip all play and happiness from a little girl? Did He not know that she would far rather have died than be left in this bare loneliness? Why did He do such things? Why? Why? And where was He? He must be somewhere; but where?

There was no answer that she heard to any of her questions, just as there had been no answer to her prayers. And yet, though so baffled, and feeling repulsed and refused, something pressed her on to seek for Him who seemed to hide Himself. Something? It was Someone: "Let Thy loving Spirit lead me forth unto the land of righteousness"—she did not pray that prayer. She did not know enough to pray so great a prayer, nor to whom to offer it, nor that there was a loving Spirit at all. But we have such an understanding God that He knows what we would say if we knew enough to say it. For, as the Tamil has it, "Thou knowest my thought in the distance. Before the word was born in my tongue, lo, Thou, O Lord, hast known it all." And so the loving Spirit, hearing the word before it was born on her tongue, led her forth to seek the land of righteousness:

> The seeker finds, none other, only he.
> The gold lies hid; the shell conceals the pearl;
> All veiled in green the rubies of the larch;
> A common stable hides the King of kings,
> The seeker finds, *none other.*

A corner of Uncrowned-King. Star's home is the two-storied white house opening on the street. The photo was taken from the attic where the boy was tied to the pillar.

One of the little sanctuaries; but the acacia bushes that used to surround the pool have been cut down for firewood, and nothing is left but the old tamarind which once dropped a pod at the feet of the little girl.

And now, moved by new thoughts, she made herself little sanctuaries where she could pray to Him whom she knew not yet: an attic in her own home; a place in her father's field among the grain before it was harvested; and in his cotton field among the low bushes with their soft floppy leaves and primrose-colored, crimson-hearted flowers. When their capsules burst and held out the white cotton-wool, she was there again. The jungle saw her too, and the tall thorn that daintily hung his mauve tassels just out of reach of the goats. But more often she found her way to the Field of the Darling-Pool. The air was scented there, for the Pool was fringed with low acacia bushes covered with perfumed yellow balls. As she thinks of it she sees the rough grass, the clumps of rushes, the shapeless, old, gnarled tamarind tree, and the Darling-Pool that looked up like a bright eye from that clustering, fragrant green.

3

Lead Us to Souls Prepared

AND while these things were so at Uncrowned-King, in an old dilapidated bungalow near the village of Great-Lake, in the taluk of Vishnu's-heaven, three people were asking for guidance. The taluk (the word is Arabian and means division of a district) is an attractive place. Greek writers of the first and second centuries speak of Korkai, one of its vanished cities. Marco Polo, who came to South India in A.D. 1292, writes of another "great and noble city"—Cail, he calls it—of the pearl fisheries on its coast, of large fish which threatened the fishery, and of "certain enchanters belonging to a class of Brahmans, who, by means of their diabolical art, prevent them from doing mischief; and as the fishing takes place in the daytime only, they discontinue the effect of the charm in the evening, in order that dishonest persons who might be inclined to take the opportunity of diving at night and stealing the oysters may be deterred by the apprehension they feel of the unrestrained ravages of these animals." Treasure is hidden in the fields of sand—old burial urns, pottery, weapons, household utensils, ornaments, and gold diadems like those found at Mycen. The talk of the people about this treasure had often set fancy flying along the roads of the past. But now we were on another quest. How find among the tens of thousands, in their scattered towns and villages, even one who would sell all that he had to buy the field wherein is hidden a more precious treasure? Where was the one, seeking goodly pearls, who for the sake of the pearl of great price would count all things as loss? "O

Lord, Thou knowest. Lead us to that one," was our prayer then, "Lover of souls, lead us to souls prepared."

• • •

Of the many places to which we went in that hot March of 1899, two stand out in clearness: a curious little settlement called the Fort on the outskirts of Vishnu's-heaven at the place where it touches the desert, and the town of Uncrowned-King, which is not far from the site of the vanished cities of long-forgotten glories.

It was early afternoon when we first saw the Fort. It was hot, but those happy little sunbirds, the children, darted about in the sunshine, or played in the doubtful shadow of the palms which border the Brahman street. There were vivid splashes of color where the little children played, otherwise the street was colorless and empty, for the people who lend it life were out of sight in the close dark of windowless rooms, trying to feel cool. To the left of where we stood, above the house tops and palms, rose the temple tower, a hundred feet of carved stone. A wall faced us, crossing the end of the street.

The wall was of clay, clumsily but massively built, rough with uneven additions and patches, the work of careless generations. It was bare and ugly, and covered, as all the world was then, with the dust of rainless months. The little flowers and grasses that had struggled for life on its ridges in the last wet season had been burnt up long ago. Only their famished shreds were left to tell how the poor wild things had tried to decorate man's prosaic. But green trees showed above it. We wondered what was inside.

A door was set deep in the wall; we knocked, but no answer came. Then friendly voices called us from doorways in the Brahman street. We sat down gratefully in the shadowy recess of a verandah, and heard that the door at which we had knocked was always locked; it had been locked years ago when a little girl had looked out on the street—a thing forbidden. She had been sawn asunder, the women said with a shudder, and buried near the door. Boys were allowed out, girls never. Boys over sixteen lived in a house apart from their mothers and sisters. Never till death did a woman go outside the walls, and even then she was not seen. She was not laid on an open bier in the usual way. She was sewn in a sack and carried to the burning ground by a door in the wall on the other side. Two such doors lay on that side. By one dead women were carried out, and by the other dead men. No townsman ever went into the Fort. All men of all castes were strictly forbidden, except the servants of the Fort, who tilled the Fort lands outside. There was no stringent law about women; but no woman known to them had ever gone in. "May we go in?" we asked.

The question came as a surprise. They had never thought of going in. And yet they had lived all their lives within sound of a laugh or a cry from the place. "Why go in? There is nothing to see. The people are not like us. They are mere animals; poor jungle creatures." Then, after a pause, came the hesitating afterthought: "Once, it is said, a white woman went in, and nothing evil befell her" as if a thought of evil had ever crossed our mind. "But this is foolish talking; you would be as a parrot watching the silk cotton pod (the pod ripens, the wind blows the fluffy seed away); for even if they let you go inside, you might wait for a lifetime and never see a woman. Each lives in her house with the door fast shut. It is hot, very hot," they repeated dissuadingly. "Why go out in such a heat?" But we went.

It was certainly hot. There was no shade. The wall seemed to concentrate heat and throb it out to us. Below, the dust scorched our feet. Above, the sky overflowed with light, a clear white blaze of heat. There is a beautiful story in the *Ramayana* (one of India's epics) which tells how Rama, Prince of Oudh, and Lakshman, his noble young brother, while journeying with their spiritual guide through forest and plain, came to an arid desert, "so hot that the tongue would scorch if it tried to describe it." But the guide taught the lads a certain charm, and as they chanted it the fiery ground changed for them into cool water-springs. We thought of this old tale then. We have a Charm by which life's glowing sand becomes a pool, and even the common fiery ground to be trodden under common feet is cooled by the Charm for us. So, hardly minding about the heat, we walked on, and came to a teakwood door fitted with huge locks and bars that looked centuries old. The door was open. We went in. A whitewashed wall built halfway across intercepted the view. We stood there for a moment and then went on past another wall, mud-built and broken, and saw trees and altars. Beyond stood a picturesque group of red-roofed houses. We had no time to see more, for before we reached the houses an old man met us, and, leading us back to the door, asked us our business.

He was a very old man. From his ears hung long gold rings. His dress was the fine white muslin of the South. His manners were those of a chief. "These tidings," he said, after listening a little, "are excellent for those outside, the ignorant people of the town. But we of the Fort are different. We require nothing external. Nor do we desire it." This for the time was final. The Fort was not open yet.

4

By a Well of Water

BUT the town of Uncrowned-King was open and our little band gathered "without the city by a well of water at the time of the evening, even the time that women go out to draw water." Soon we had a crowd of men at one side of the large well; the other side they left open for the women who came with their water vessels, let down their palm leaf baskets, drew up the water, poured it into their vessels and moved off without taking much notice of us. The splash of the water hardly seemed to matter in that wide open air. It did not distract our hearers, so it did not disturb us. And we searched the faces before us to find the face of a seeker. Presently some children came, each with her polished brass water pot under her arm. Among them was a little girl—the child of the Field of the Darling-Pool and the little sanctuaries.

She had come to draw water as usual. She had left home with only one thought, to fill her water vessel. But seeing the crowd she lingered to watch and listen. She had never seen foreigners before.

"There were three white people, six Tamil people, a talking noise, a singing noise and a box which made a noise." That was the first impression produced by ourselves, our fellow workers, our baby organ and our ardent singing.

Presently she moved away. Her mother would not like her to delay. Then a madman came and tried to disturb the meeting. "See the white man beat the madman!" shouted the crowd with enthusiasm. This would be too good to miss. She stopped and watched. But the white man only put his arm on the madman's shoulder and drew him gently out of the crowd, while the Indian brother continued speaking. This was a tame proceeding. She was about to go when a sentence repeated several times by the preacher caught her attention: *"There is a living God. There is a living God: He turned me, a lion, into a lamb."*

Then, with the sudden gladness of a new discovery, a revelation, it flashed upon her that here at last was the answer to her question—the question that had been pushed into the background of her mind by her sorrow over her little brother. The God who could change a lion-man into a lamb, the God who could change dispositions, was the God of gods, the Sovereign God, Creator. Him she would worship henceforth, Him and no other. To speak of Him as living implied that other gods were dead. "I will not worship a dead god," she almost spoke aloud in her eagerness. "Siva is a dead god. I will not rub his ashes on my forehead." Then she went slowly home, pondering those luminous words: *"There is a living God: there is a living God."*

She did not want to sleep that night. She wanted to lie awake and speak with the living God. Does it sound unbelievable? But who can explain a spiritual revelation? The soul of the child had surprised the secret of eternal happiness.

And we read in our camp that evening (it was March 16): "I heard a voice from heaven, as the voice of many waters, and as the voice of a great thunder; and I heard the voice of harpers harping with their harps."

5

I am the Ground of thy Beseeching

BUT memory, arbitrary, selective, picks out a few threads from the texture of that night, and I see them lying before me. They are as it were yellow, a dull yellow-ochre color, for that was the color of the lining of our tents in those days. That color, or even more quickly and surely the stuffy smell of canvas that has been packed up for weeks and is not properly aired, can recall a memory of heaviness, the oppression of the enemy. What had our preaching done? A crowd of men, some women, many children had gathered and listened quietly and then melted back into the streets of their little town without a question or a single sign of interest. Heaven, hell, sin, holiness, what did those great words mean to them?

> Hearing their one hope with an empty wonder,
> Dimly contented with a show of things.

It had been like that. We had prayed to be led to souls prepared; we had not, so far as we knew, found one yet. It mattered tremendously that these people who were so near us now, and yet so far away, should know the true God and Jesus Christ whom He had sent. Nothing else really mattered. And thoughts of India's millions who are as though the Savior of the world had never died on Calvary, had never risen, was never to return, swept over me. And thoughts came too of the unrecognized love of Him who said, "All day long I have stretched forth My hands," and of the Voice which crieth without in the streets, in the chief places of concourse, in the opening of the gates, by the well side of town and village, by this well side this evening, "Turn you, I will make known My words unto you;" and so few heard, so few turned, so few cared to know those words, and I was sorrowful, never dreaming that in the town nearby, that night, there was a child who could not sleep for awe and wonder.

I am the Ground of thy beseeching, wrote Julian of Norwich. *First it is my will that thou have it; and after, I make thee to will it; and after, I make thee to beseech it and thou beseechest it. How should it then be that thou shouldst not have thy beseeching? . . . Therefore He saith thus: Pray inwardly, though thee thinketh it savour thee not: for it is profitable, though thou feel not, though thou see nought; yea, though thou think thou canst not. For in dryness and in barrenness, in sickness and in feebleness, then is thy prayer well-pleasant to Me, though thee thinketh it savour thee nought but little. And so is all thy believing prayer in my sight.*

Most of us find ourselves at times in the midst of the Valley where the pilgrim had to walk, where, ever and anon, flame and smoke come out in abundance, with sparks and hideous noises, things that care not for our sword. And there are doleful voices there, and rushings to and fro, and all this goes on for several miles together. But if we use the weapon called *All prayer* (praying when we feel most prayerless, for "God accepteth the good will and the travail of His servant, howsoever we feel") and if we walk on in the strength of the Lord God, those fiends of the Valley will give back and come no further.

To look up into a dark sky and see it suddenly open, as lightning plays across it, to see in one revealing flash deep into the kingdoms of light, is to know what prayer most truly is. There is mystery, but beyond that darkness is not a deeper darkness, but light—kingdoms of light.

6

The First of Three

BEFORE the seed of life was sown in the heart of that little girl by the well side she had been carefully considering our small company. We often wish we knew what was in the minds of those who see us for the first time. (No Englishwoman had ever been there before that evening, and rarely an Englishman.) This is what was in the child's mind: the two elder white people were evidently husband and wife, and she wondered why this was so. They appeared to be devoted to their God, but they looked happy. The devoted, so her Hindu mind argued, are ascetics and do not look happy. This puzzled her for a while. They must have married before they became devotees, and could not change now, she thought with compassion, for she was sure they must be sorry about it. Dear saints, they have been together in the heavenly land for many a year. I am rather glad they never heard this artless tale. But, after all, if they had, they would have smiled, for they understood the land.

> The narrow thorny path he trod,
>   "Enter into My joy," said God.
> The sad ascetic shook his head ;
>   "I've lost all taste for joy," he said.

That might have been written in India.

And then a startling thought crossed the mind of this little girl. She knew that her parents would not allow her to worship the living God, whom she had instantly recognized to be the

God for whom she had been searching and to whom her heart had as instantly gone out with a sense of possession and peace, for was He not the Answer to her questions? Then she must go to those strangers. There was no other way. For she must worship Him; she must learn how to worship Him; and who could teach her that except those who were His worshippers? And she studied the three carefully that she might be able to decide to whom she would go. (She never thought of one of the four Indian women as being able to receive her or protect her. It must be one of the three white people who would help her.) She settled on the youngest, who was in a sari, a little detail that somehow made her feel "near in mind, and a spring like a spring of water was opened in me." This is how she wrote of those first swift impressions in that vivid little story in the notebook: "and the spring overflowed in love for that ammal in the sari, and as I looked at her I knew that if only I could go to her, she would have a place in her heart for me." And she thought: "This living God, who is God of gods, is strong enough to do anything. Nothing can be difficult to Him. He can do a wonderful thing, even though I cannot understand how He can do it. He can do it very wonderfully, I think; He will cause the day to come that will bring us together, and she will be my mother and I will be her daughter, and she will teach me to worship Him. And she and I will go out to speak of Him to others as she does now."

It was in this simple way and with words as simple as these that the field was bought and the pearl. (I know that those immortal stories carry another interpretation, but a single Scripture is rich enough to carry several, and nothing could more powerfully and yet tenderly show just what happens when a searching soul finds its treasure; for joy thereof it goeth and selleth all that it hath and buyeth that field. And like the pearl merchant, who when he had found one pearl of great price went and sold all that he had and bought it, it counts all things but loss for that excellency.)

Next morning to the happy child the world looked different, and she danced as she walked. As she was under twelve years old she was free to go where she would, except, of course, to defiling places, as her people would have called a low-caste house or our Christian camp.

That morning we of the women's band went out to visit in the town. We were called into many houses belonging to the ruling clan which was that of the happy child. And soon she joined the troop of children who attached themselves to us like a long and vigorously wagging tail; and she followed us from house to house. The last house to which we went was in a quarter of the town considered low caste by her people, so when she returned home she was sharply scolded and told to change her sari. To touch it would have been pollution to them.

But that evening found her again on the edge of the crowd near the demon shrine. (Once a year, before that shrine, the devotee drank warm blood as it flowed from the neck of the newly slain victim.) They were a rough and turbulent set there, and the noise drowned our voices so that she could not hear. Perhaps the parents knew of her disappointment, for they did not say much in rebuke when she returned rather dejectedly home. They probably thought that she had learned her lesson.

It was different when she went to the Christian camp. She remembers every minute of that time. She sat on the floor of our tent among other children and repeated a song after us. The poetry to which she was accustomed was difficult to understand, and our song struck her as singularly easy. But her heart was "like a little room," so she described it afterwards; it could not hold much then. Only she understood that the living God heard when we prayed; "This entering in made a space for itself." We knew nothing of the earnest little listener, did not even notice her among the others, for she kept in the background shyly and ran home without speaking to us.

And as she ran home she resolved that she would test the living God. She would pray three prayers. If two out of three were answered (by answered, she meant that if exactly what she asked were granted) then she would be sure that He heard when we called, and that the living God was God of gods indeed. And so she would prove and know the certainty of the words of truth.

When she got home, her mother was standing on the doorstep with a broom of knotted grass in her hand. This meant punishment. Quick as thought she prayed: "O living God, do not let my mother beat me. O living God, answer this first of three!"

Her mother caught her by the arm. "Where hast thou been, thou naughty one? Oh, perverse one, come here! Thou hast been to those low-caste people. Chee!" Was the stinging swish of the broom the answer to her prayer?

But she kept quiet. Would not something happen, something worth waiting for? "Those low-caste people have perverted thee already!" exclaimed her mother, mistaking the quietness for sullenness. "Verily thou hast no feeling: I must give thee a double punishment." Then indeed, bewildered, for to find "the first of three" collapse like a burst soap bubble was shattering, the perverse one broke into bitter sobs, and she cried herself to sleep that night. The whole household was angry with her. She had disgraced her caste.

7

Two Out of Three

AND yet next day she went to the camp again, forgetting everything save that she was hungry and would find food there, and she was thirsty and there she would find drink.

So she sat down among the other children, an inconspicuous child. She was not the only one in bird-bright colors, and in that crowd was just one of many. But she listened, as perhaps no other did that day, to the loveliest story in all the world. And then a song was sung line by line in the Tamil way, each line being repeated by the chorus of children.

And while the song was being sung something happened under the yellow-ochre roof of that tent. How put it tenderly enough to be true? "The Lord hath appeared of old unto me, saying, Yea, I have loved thee with an everlasting love: therefore with loving-kindness have I drawn thee." The disappointment of yesterday was forgotten. Love drew the child. She followed. Love embraced her. She yielded herself to that embrace.

And then to her surprise she heard a question asked, "Has any child been punished for coming to hear about Jesus Lord?" (for so we say it in Tamil). She kept still, but the other children knew of her trouble; they had tried to dissuade her from coming lest there should be more beating; and one of them answered for her. "If that should be again, then let the one who is beaten say over and over the Name of Jesus Lord, looking up to Him inwardly, and He will give patience to endure, and He will give peace and comfort." This was the answer to which that little seeker eagerly listened. She would not forget the name, *Jesus Lord.*

The children's meeting broke up as usual. The merry little people salaamed and ran off, and as I committed that morning's sowing to the Master of the field, the child who had listened so keenly was running along the road repeating over and over, as though charmed by the very name, *"Jesus Lord, Jesus Lord."* Verily there is enchantment in that Name, the Name that is above every name.

The child ran on, and as she murmured that dear Name to herself it dawned upon her that it must be the Name of the living God. This reminded her of her test. Two prayers still remained out of three. She went to the Field of the Darling-Pool and stood underneath the tamarind tree; the ripe fruit hung low. It is stealing to gather fruit; but you may eat it if it falls of itself. "O Jesus Lord, living God, make the fruit to fall." And a pod fell at her feet.

She picked it up. Did ever the rough brown pod of a tamarind tree say so much to anyone before? Out of two prayers the second had been answered immediately. All now depended upon what would happen to the third. If it found the ear of Jesus Lord, then He was without doubt the God for whom she had been searching so long.

It was twilight now. She was not allowed to be out alone after dark, so, a little anxiously, she ran quickly down the street to her home. "Living God, Jesus Lord, deign to listen; do not let my mother punish me." Her heart beat fast as she reached the doorstep of her father's house. The door was open and her mother stood there waiting. The broom was not in her hand. "Come in, child, I thought thou wert lost," she said, and she drew her in, and, ladling out some hot curry and rice into a brass bowl, called her to supper. So the question was settled. Jesus Lord was the living God. He heard prayer: two prayers out of three had been answered. He loved her. She did not know at all how that could be, but it was true. She had proved and now she knew the certainty of the words of truth. Him she would love and worship and serve all her life long. And in an ardor of joy she turned to Him whom she had found at last. This was the child whom we were to call Arulai Tara, Star of Grace, when, some months later, she was given to us. From the first day she was an ardent little lover.

"They asked the Lover: 'What thing is farthest from thy heart?' He answered, 'Indifference.' 'And why so?' 'Because nearest to my heart is love, which is the contrary of indifference.'" And so it was with Star.

8

Star is Sent to Learn Sense

ONE of our Tamil proverbs declares that to speak truth is to offend those whose eyesight is defective. Far from the thoughts of that little girl was any such rapier thrust as this, but she could not avoid giving offence. On a projection of the big carved doorway of her home was a small basket in which the sacred ashes were kept (token of the worship of Siva). These ashes must daily be smeared on the brow, arms, and breast of every devout Saivite man; women and girls must smear them on the forehead. To refuse to do so was to declare oneself superior to one's ancestors, a renegade, an outsider. Star could not smear the ashes now. She did not know what it was that hindered the performance of this and many like observances. She only knew that they were impossible to her. She had found the living God. She had even less to help her than her sister Mimosa had in later years. No old woman came to her and said: "He will never forsake you, He has never forsaken me. He will wonderfully lead you. In every least thing He will wonderfully lead you." No one said anything at all except that she was bewitched. With a child's frank faith she had declared herself a worshipper of the living God, using the word that had caught her attention at the well, and, naturally enough, this word was most offensive. Was Siva, then, a *dead* God? And who was she to say it or imply it?

But Star knew that the roof above her had opened, or a window had opened there, and a voice had spoken to her and called her. Who would not follow who had heard Him call?

So through all the entanglement of voices she followed. The trouble of her questions had fallen from her. She knew now who could change dispositions, and that He, the living God, had appeared to her in the tent as the loving God too. This had sweetened all her thought about her little brother, though she still longed to know for certain where he had gone, for he was as alive and dear to her as the day he had last looked up at her with laughing eyes. And carefully gathering up all she could remember of what she had heard in the tent with the yellow-ochre roof, she held it close to her heart, and when things became too difficult she would steal away to one or another of her little sanctuaries and speak her thoughts to Him who was her living God. She had never heard proper prayer—prayer, I mean, set in formal phrases. What she had heard in that little meeting in the tent had only been the simplest and most direct speech with our heavenly Father; and so she spoke as a child would, just as she felt: "O living God, take me to that ammal in the sari. I am not allowed to live as Your follower in my father's house. I cannot wait till I am grown up. I cannot live so long without knowing more of You. If You do not take me quickly I shall die without You; then where will Your power be? How shall I be sure that You are indeed the living God?" (Yes, even after the sign of two answers out of three, and the quick uprush of love, the fear would sometimes come again.) "O living God, show Your power and Your livingness by taking me to that ammal in the sari while I am young. Take me away from my people to Your people. If You who created me cannot do this for me, who can?" Does it sound irreverent? She did not mean it so. "O living God, do me the favor (the Tamil for *please*), take me to the ammal in the sari soon."

I pause here, wondering how I can show what a great thing this child was asking. But I fear that I cannot. Such a thing had never happened in the history of her caste. The rocks and steeps of the impossible stood up round about her, closed her in on every side, and she never heard anyone say, "Over rocks that are steepest Love will find out the way."

When there is no place
For the glowworm to lie,
When there is no space
For receipt of a fly;
When the midge dares not venture
Lest herself fast she lay,
If Love come, he will enter
And will find out the way.

All this was an unknown world of thought to her, but the kind of prayer that was a continual laying of her longings at the feet of her new-found Lord became the habit of her soul. In the children's meeting in the tent something had been said which she never forgot; it was about talking with God at any time: "He will always listen and always understand; even if we do not for a little while hear Him answer us, we must not be discouraged; the ear of our soul has to learn to hear. If He does not say *Yes* to something we are asking, but *Wait*, or *No*, we must not be impatient and unhappy, as though it meant He did not care. The one sure thing is that He hears, and cares. If we listen carefully, sooner or later we shall hear Him speaking softly and very comfortingly in our hearts." "So," wrote that child in after days, "I talked with Him everywhere I went."

But the clamor of the noise of words grew more persistent and emphatic. Star's mother and sister and her womenfolk in general were sure now that she was bewitched. How else account for such infatuation? It was preposterous. Those people who came and talked by the well side had cast a spell upon her. She was bewitched, spellbound.

Her maternal uncle lived in a village within a day's walk. He was a kindly, friendly man, a Christian (I know the surprise in the word, but so it was) who had never caused a disturbing ripple to affect the family life of the clan; except that once, in a moment of delusion, he had permitted a ceremony called Spiritual Washing to be performed upon him. It was, however, the mere sprinkling of pure water on the head. Some such rite was daily performed, and much more thoroughly, by every orthodox Hindu. Like all his relatives he carefully kept caste and custom. He did not eat food cooked by a Christian of a lower caste than his, so he was not defiled. He could enjoy a Hindu festival with his relatives, he was not in the least cut off from the life of the clan, and he never dreamed of troubling them with any private fancies of his own. Where he lived there were many Christians. Let this foolish child see them. Then she would learn sense, said her father.

9

Like Blue Sky in a Storm at Sea

SO to her uncle's home Star went, fulfilled with grateful joy. She would be with Christians. "But when I was among them, I saw that these Christians were quite different from what I had thought that they would be," is a disillusioned word from the note-book. Her father's wisdom was justified. Gradually her first impressions and fervor of desire faded.

And yet there was at least one true Christian in that village (the juicy one, the people called her, meaning that she was full of sap; there are such, thank God, in the driest places), but she was very old and Star may not have seen her. One night when a slight earthquake shock startled the village, the Christians thought that it was the herald of our Lord's return and they rushed off to old Blessing's house. If she were gone then they would know that the Lord had come and taken her and left them behind. They found her at home, however, fast asleep, and, much relieved, went back to bed.

There was a little mission school in the village, which Star was allowed to attend. As she was only a beginner she was put in the infants' class, where they learned the same text every day for a week. But the teacher let her sit by her when she taught the older children.

"One day she was teaching about the Creation. She said, 'On the fourth day God made the sun, moon and stars.' I asked her, 'Sister, how did the people know what time it was by night or day, and how did they know it was the first, second or third day, before the sun and moon came?' She said that the people had clocks, and by those clocks they knew. I thought, How wonderful! The clocks came before the sun and moon. I never forgot that wonder."

Her teacher, in the kindness of her heart, used to take off her jewels and press them on Star to wear as a loan for the sake of friendliness. At first she refused, but after a little while she wore them to please her teacher. One day, when the teacher was taking off her jewels and putting them in Star's ears, she found that there were not enough holes, so she wanted to make a new hole. To this Star agreed; the teacher pierced her ear with a thorn and plastered it with lime to make it heal quickly.

Star's uncle, however, objected. "If thy father hears of it he will be displeased. He will say I let thee run wild; he will come and take thee away." Poor little Star, who had not given up her desire to serve the living God, though her high hopes had collapsed, was torn between the fear of hurting her teacher's feelings by what would seem ungraciousness, and the fear that her father would take her away from the place where she had a chance to learn. So she spent a miserable night, "with heart fearing and ear aching, for the thorn was still fixed in it." Next morning her father came.

Star ran to him with an eager defence of her uncle. It was her fault, not his; he did not let her run wild. "O father, forgive me," she pleaded. "Do not take me away from my uncle." But her father was perplexed, for he had heard nothing "of the lime-washed ear matter." And when at last he did understand, a slow smile crept round his mouth and his shrewd eyes regarded her with grim satisfaction.

He took the trouble to go to the teacher and thank her for influencing his foolish child in the right direction. "Her mind became quite changed," he said apologetically, "after she saw the three white people and the four Indian women at the well."

And Star heard, and over her rushed the longings that had filled her heart that first evening, and she pulled the thorn out of her ear, wishing that she could take off her own little jewels, the simple gold necklet and earrings of a child, as a sign for all to see that her allegiance was fixed on something and on Someone out of sight. But that would anger her father, and he would take her home, so she restrained herself. Nothing, however, could persuade her to give in again to the jewel play; not even to please her kind teacher would she submit to the decoration of ears and nose and neck, and every part of her person upon which something could be hung. From that day she "became hungry for God's word." The hunger grew and spread in her heart like a burning fire. Sometimes she did not know what to do or where to go, and often the thought of that ammal in the sari came to her mind. "Oh, I wish I knew where she is! I would run to her if I knew"—that was her constant thought.

A banked-up fire may smoulder, but it can burn hotly, and at last Star could no longer smother her longing for spiritual food. She asked her uncle to tell her about the true God. "But what is the good of telling thee about the true God?" was his crushing reply. "Thy father is going to marry thee to a heathen (literally, wisdomless one) next year, and thou wilt be a heathen for ever." The cold finality of the words appalled Star. She felt it the more because she knew that it was indeed her father's intention to do this very thing. She did not answer her uncle, but that night, "with her heart full of tears and fears," she poured out her prayer to her living God. "O God, listen to me again. I beseech You listen to me. Can You not do a wonderful thing before next year? Am I going to be a heathen for ever? To be married to a heathen is not my desire. To be a heathen for ever is not my desire. Oh, will You not do a wonderful thing before next year? Please, please, open a way for me before next year; please save me, please take me to that ammal in the sari, whom I saw by the well, and tell her to take me for her own child, and teach me about You. Amen." And after that she slept in peace.

grass, so was that hour to Star. But she had to wait for two more days, a few hours more than that indeed, for we should arrive home on Saturday evening, and she could not hope to see us till Sunday. She would go to the temple of the Christians and see us there. The time was counted by heart throbs, but the hour came at last. She could not have told anyone the thoughts that filled her mind as she left her uncle's house that Sunday morning and set forth on her great adventure. As she walked she remembered, what in the excitement of the moment she had forgotten, that she had no offering. A Hindu never approaches a temple without an offering. She stopped, and asked her living God to give her something to give, and immediately saw a copper coin lying on the soft, deep sand. She picked it up gratefully, and polished it on her sari until it shone. Her heart was full of a tender sweetness.

It was on this deep soft sand the copper coin lay ready for Star to find.

Just so had the pod of the tamarind tree in the Field of the Darling-Pool fallen at her feet. The living God was indeed near and very kind. She wondered at His kindness and yet was not surprised. Nor need we be surprised; for there is nothing that our Father will not do to help the faith of His young children. Later it may be different. Tamarind pods do not always fall from the tree for us. The silver and the gold we so much need do not lie on the path for us to pick up as we walk in difficult ways. To us is a new joy then, and a deeper: we are trusted to trust our Father when all that we hear Him say is this: "Blessed is he whosoever shall not be offended in Me." But for the heart that knows Him, it is enough.

Soon after finding that coin, Star reached the church. One quick glance round as she walked demurely up the empty space between the men on the right and the women on the left showed her what she had hoped to see. She knelt down among the village children sitting in rows on the floor and prayed, "My living God, that ammal is there by the pillar, the one whom I saw by the well. She is just behind me. She and I are in Your temple. How wonderful it is! You who have brought us both so near to each other, show her, please, how I love her, and how I want to be a Christian, and want to be her child. Amen."

10

Between Lovers There is Recognition

OF all this story of desire I knew nothing that Sunday morning as I went as usual to the village church, and sat on the floor by a pillar, without the slightest flicker of anticipation of anything unusual happening.

Presently I noticed, kneeling in front of me, a little stranger. It was the arch of her foot, as I saw it from behind as she knelt, that caught my attention; it reminded me of John Ridd's Lorna Doone. Who was she, this little bird of a different feather, who was so friendly with the other little birds, and yet so evidently not one of them? Something moved me to want her beside me. A bright-eyed bird of the village with a child's quick intuition noticed this, and touched her, whispering in her ear. She rose at once, and nestled close to me as one to whom the place belonged. "Some of love's secrets reveal others, and therefore between lovers there is recognition:" from that day, though separated many a time in the flesh, we have never been apart for one moment in spirit. And as she looked into my eyes with one long earnest look, I, meeting those earnest eyes, so serious yet so shining, for they were alight with a joy and a contentment that I should later understand, felt that the God of loving surprises was giving something very dear to me; and with both hands I took His gift and held it up to Him to bless.

Then, for still I did not know who she was or that she had heard before, she says that I began to tell her of the love of our Lord Jesus Christ.

All this time the church bell had been ringing steadily with a kind of polite, "Come, come; please come" in its tone; but now it hurried into a vehement and rapid, "Come, come at once." And with that the pastor and the missionary walked up the aisle. But the child was too absorbed to notice them; she was recalled to her surroundings by the voice of the old pastor—a dear old saint known everywhere as "the pastor who never tells a lie." (This was not intended as a reflection on others, but signified that he had been tried and not found wanting.) He opened the service with a phrase which literally means, "Let us silently repeat incantations in worship according to prescribed forms, and with accompanying ceremonies"; but it has been Christianized into, "Let us pray," and as she had lately been with Christians, Star understood it in this sense. The prayer, however, was beyond her. It had not been framed for little Hindu girls, but for instructed Christians. And though a well-read Hindu or Muslim might follow, as one did lately in our House of Prayer, interjecting "Quite so. Excellent!" as approved petitions were presented, it was only a sort of holy patter to such as Star. Then a lyric was sung or droned to a musical composition, which appeared to have lost its way and to be wandering about trying to find a place to stop. Star did not mind this; India is patient. Psalms were read, alternate verses by pastor and congregation; this was most exhilarating, for the schoolboys raced the old pastor, and often began their verses before he had finished his.

And so the service proceeded, till there was a pause, when plates were passed up and down the rows, and Star realized that this was the time for giving the gift that her living God had laid on the sand for her. This done, she saw a white man stand forth in front of the people; he was the one whom she had seen by the well. He spoke about sin and the punishment of sin, and finished with God's great love and the salvation that has been prepared for men. She did not understand all he said, but she understood these chief things.

After the service we went to the bungalow together; Star, quivering with expectation, waited for the words she longed to hear; she was sure that I would say, "Stay with me, and be my child," and was sorely disappointed because I said nothing like that. A few days later the longing that was in her conquered her shyness, and she told me of her prayer and of her expectation. She was not prepared to hear that, though no one could hinder her from loving her Lord and being loved by Him (and so being in very truth His own), she "could not choose her religion," as her people would say, or decide with whom she would live, till she was eighteen. But would her parents wait till she was eighteen before they gave her away in marriage?

Very early in the story of this child the words of the three who refused to fear had to be taught and learned, "If it be so, our God whom we serve is able to deliver us from the burning fiery furnace, and he will deliver us out of thine hand, O king. *But if not...*" We left it at that.

Of all the questions that crowded the mind of this little girl the most urgent was, "Where is my baby brother?" The Tamil has no word quite like our *heaven*. How could it? Heaven is a word of revelation. It can say "Other world," but the word connotes only other; not other and blissfully happy. "What a singing life is there. There is not a dumb bird in all that large field"—of this it knows nothing. *Release* is the word that comes nearest that which eye hath not seen nor heart conceived, but even Release falls far, far short of what our youngest children picture when they say "heaven." Still, it is a peaceful word; it means liberty from the chain of the body; and the body, in Hindu thought, is more than this body of our humiliation, it is a fetter.

So when, the first time we were out in the moonlight together, Star, after gazing in silence into the pure brightness of the sky, asked me where a Hindu baby goes when it dies. "Does it attain Release?" She meant, "Does it go to heaven?"

I did not know then of the baby brother, but I answered as anyone would, I think, who knew the Lover of little children. We were quiet again for a while; and thoughts filled the quietness. What flocks of little white birds must be flying through the air every hour of night and day. The sun as he goes, "always trailing a sunset behind him, and pushing a sunrise on before," does not stay the flight of those birds, nor does the silver moon; there they fly, like doves to their windows. And we thought of them too, as lambs folded by Death, who, like the Good Shepherd Himself, gathers the lambs in his arm and carries them in his bosom to Love's own Country. In the days to come we were often to stand together in the still, green place we call God's Garden, and sing with a sure hope:

Out of the heat and out of the rain,
Never to know of sin or pain,
Never to fall and never to fear,
Could we wish better for one so dear?

What has he seen and what has he heard?
He who has flown away like a bird?
Eye has not seen, nor dream can show
All he has seen, all he may know.

For the pure powers of Calvary
Bathe little souls in innocency;
Tender, tender Thy love-words be,
"Dear little child, come home to Me."

11

A Story-song

AND now, knowing how precarious such an opportunity as this was, I took her directly to the heart of all things, the Cross. I cannot forget that hour. We were in the room where I was soon to know an extremity of grief for her, an extremity of prayer. We were on our knees together, and I was reading slowly to her from the nineteenth chapter of the Gospel of St. John, when the Spirit of Truth, who does indeed take of the things of Christ and show them unto us, drew near and "shewed" that "grievous setting of the Garland of thorns unsparingly and without pity," and the other manifold pains of those tortured hours; till suddenly it became too much to bear.

How can the soul of Christendom be numb to it all? Star's soul was not numb. When we came to the words, *"Where they crucified Him,"* she could refrain no longer. "Is it all over?" she cried, and her face was wet with tears; "will they never hurt Him again?" And we drew a deep breath of relief—"They will never hurt Him again."

After this came, for the first time, what old writers call a sense of sin, and I know of no better way to describe it. This child who had sought for God and found Him—had been found by Him, rather—now began to understand how much more was meant by being a Christian than she had at first understood, and so she came at last to something that I can best show by writing a story-song made for a later generation of children to help them deeper into the words, "If any man will open the door I will come in."

First the child speaks:

> Dear Lord Jesus, will You come
> Into such a little home?
>
> It is poor and it is bare,
> Dear Lord, You'll find nothing there.
>
> It is very dusty too;
> Oh, it isn't fit for You.
>
> Not a flower has bloomed for me,
> There's no fruit upon my tree.
>
> And, Lord Jesus, have You heard?
> I have not one singing bird.
>
> Dearest Lord, how can You come
> Into such a dismal home?

Then the Lord answers:

> But, My child, I want to come,
> Want to make your house My home.
>
> If I come it shall be fair,
> In and out and everywhere.
>
> I will clear the dust away,
> Make it clean and make it gay.
>
> All its flowers will bloom for Me,
> Fruit will ripen on your tree.
>
> In your garden will be heard
> Many a merry singing bird.
>
> Dearest child, I want to come.
> May I make your house My home?

And at last the child says,

> O my Savior, Lord and King,
> Come, I give You everything.
>
> With my whole heart I say, Come;
> Come and make my house Your home.

It may well be that my story so far has appeared too full of flashes of insight to be truly the story of a child, even an Indian child; and yet it is true. The soul of a child is a delicately-tuned instrument, and the hands of God can strike what chords He will on it. But it is true, too, that there was a gradual opening of the understanding, and the simple words of the children's song show this. After all, picture-words are, like pictures, figures of the true.

For several weeks, whose hours were as coined gold to us both, Star was allowed to come daily to the bungalow for teaching. Her parents thought of this teaching as *puddypu* (spelled so as to give the sound of that most convenient word, which means study, learning). There is not much danger, so at least it is believed, that anything obnoxious will find its way in. Star's parents approved of her having puddypu. But soon it was evident that much more than that was being absorbed. And suddenly she was snatched away.

12

Black Sand

WHAT is it that causes some minutes to be preserved as though they were of singular preciousness? They are like the various sands that we find at Cape Comorin, jet-black, white, and often so colored and so bright that some playful giant might have been powdering jewels deep under the sea, and flinging them up in handfuls with every tide. Our children pour these sands into a glass so that they may see them more clearly, and I think that is what happens to these minutes. They are poured into some slight clear glass like a wineglass on its slender stem, and the years make no difference to those grains in the glass; black, white, colored, they are imperishable.

I see some grains now, black with a quick and dreadful fear, for Star, summoned by her parents, had run across from her uncle's house to tell me that she must go home, but only for four days. She was aglow with pleasure. There would be much to tell her mother and sisters—she had forgotten for the moment that they might not care to hear. "I shall read from my Gospel to them," she said, pulling the little book from a fold in her sari, for she could spell the words out now, "I shall tell them the beautiful stories," and she danced on one foot, then on the other. There was something of the gaiety of a bird about her that day: gay garments, the minivet-color still, crimson and orange like that tiny bird's plumage; bright eyes, the freshness of childhood—how could she fear? She would soon be back. Of course she would soon be back.

But my heart feared. Grain by grain, black sands dropped into the glass. The parents had determined to withdraw her from our influence. The "feeling which is evidence" told me it was so.

But no; the bright minivet turned at the door, "Only four days and I shall be back," and then, turning again to gather up kisses in her fingers in the Tamil way and blow them to me, she was gone.

And before she had reached her home we heard that she would never be allowed to come back.

People tried to comfort me; words, words—it was all words, a wind of words, their comfort, chaff; and what is chaff to the wheat? Such talk did not pierce through the skin of grief, much less find the way to its heart. I shut myself up in the only room that can be shut up in a South Indian bungalow—my bathroom, and was thankful for that room. The feel of the East is in the story of Joseph when he yearned upon his brother, and though apparently his chamber was not all open windows and doors, as ours are, still here we have it: "And Joseph made haste: and he sought where to weep; and he entered into his chamber, and wept there. And he washed his face, and went out, and refrained himself."

13

By What He Conquers

A WEEK crawled past and we heard nothing. Star would have sent a message had she not been prevented. We knew of one who, for a less fault than hers, had been kept in chains for three years. If chains were in question now, any move on our part would only rivet them the more firmly. We could do nothing for her but pray and pray again.

Then we heard that she had been forced to obey. A family council had been called. They had mocked the little lonely girl. She had been ordered to worship the idol she used to serve, and rub Siva's ashes on her forehead. She had refused, and been severely punished. She had held out bravely at first, but at last it was too much for her, and she had bowed to the idol, rubbed on the ashes. She would soon be married and sent far away. And all this was told, not as rumor, but as certainty. And she knew so little, so very little. This was the cry within me then. She did not know enough to know that "full preciously our Lord keepeth us when it seemeth to us that we are near forsaken."

As our bullock cart rumbled home over the road from the town where we had heard it, there was time to feel it. Everything seemed to feel it too. Great-Lake, as we skirted the water, blazed in a still white fire of pain. The cart wheels ground it out of the sand. "Although the fig tree shall not blossom, neither shall fruit be in the vines; the labor of the olive shall fail, and the fields shall yield no meat; the flock shall be cut off from the fold, and there shall be no herd in the stalls: Yet I will rejoice in the Lord, I will joy in the God of my salvation": I had often read these words of uttermost faith, I had given them to others. They were given to me to put upon the wall. But never till we watch "the terrible and fiery finger shrivel the falsehood" from our soul do we discover how far we may be from plain honesty. It is easier to put a text on a wall than to live in the spirit of it.

But we never come to the end of the tender mercies of our Lord. Those three sad miles behind the trotting bulls led straight to Rutherford's "Had I known what He was keeping for me, I should never have been so fainthearted." Faith's eyes, he says—God give us such eyes—"can see through a gloom of God, and under it read His thoughts of love and peace," His beautiful thoughts to usward which have been ever of old. We little know what He is preparing for us, perhaps round the next corner of the road.

On an earlier page I told of a night made heavy by the oppression of the enemy. This was not only because of apparent failure at Uncrowned-King, but because things generally were discouraging just then. Many doors had been closed to us after the conversion of two caste girls in the Great-Lake district. Any young man or woman who was suspected of interest in the teaching had been spirited away. It was partly this which had made our little Star such a jewel of joy. All round us was a neighborhood which had become like a rock at low tide studded with limpet shells. Limpet wise, each coterie resented the lightest touch on its shell, and showed its feelings by fastening the firmer on the rock. Those were the days when our appearance in the most offended villages brought handfuls of dust, thrown from behind walls, full in our faces. We did not mind the dust, but we did mind being shut out of the people's hearts. And yet we could not wonder at them. From their point of view it was the only thing to do. And we came to understand what Meredith Townsend meant when he wrote of the tenacity of will which, coexistent as it is with a surface flexibility, so often perplexes us. "The will of an Asiatic, once fairly roused, closes on its purpose with a grip to which nothing in the mind of a European can compare—a grip which seems too strong for the conscience, the judgment, and even the heart. The man is like one possessed, and cannot, even if he would, change his self-appointed course."

About that time a young Brahman barrister, whose interest in books had brought us into touch with him, came to see us and remonstrated with us for receiving converts whose caste had forbidden them to have dealings with us. It would be to the end, he said, not peace, but a sword. We were feeling very sad about this ourselves, and we besought him to use his influence towards winning liberty of conscience for his people. "Why should they not be Christians at home, as in China and Japan?" we urged, fired with a sudden hope that this man, who quoted the English poets in every second sentence, this platform orator, newspaper writer, social reformer, would come to the rescue, and in his own house at least do something persuasive and brave. He stared at us, amazed; the hate in his eyes stabbed us. Then with a concentration of scorn we shall never forget, he spoke the truth to us, "Liberty of conscience? Christians at home? There is absolutely nothing we would not do to prevent such a thing occurring." The will had closed there.

But it is by what He conquers that the power of Christ is to be discovered. When the battle is joined, "the first result is a great exhibition of Satanic power. Satan's power to be manifested must be assaulted. *It is by what He conquers that Christ's power is to be discovered.*"

14

Wind

AND now the winds were blowing upon our little girl. One glance at her father's face had told her all. She was not to return. He had heard that she wanted to be a Christian. This must be stopped. When he said that her faith and courage, she thought, flew away; and it was as though (this is her own word) she had been dropped into a deep muddy pit. Perhaps her faith and courage had not flown very far, for on the next day, Sunday, she found her way to the small schoolroom to which in after years Mimosa was to go, and where a young school teacher held a feeble attempt at a service for the very few and very ignorant and indifferent poor folk who came. It was for her the burning of her boats, Crusader-fashion: there could be no retreat now. It was the throwing down of her ladder, as Philip of Macedon threw down the ladders set against the wall of the assaulted city lest his soldiers should climb down; it meant that she was committed to the uttermost. Her father understood her action to mean this, and it enraged him. His dignity forbade him to go to the Christian schoolroom and call her out; he waited for her at home.

> Across the will of nature
>   Leads on the path of God ;
> Not where the flesh delighteth
>   The feet of Jesus trod.

Not where the flesh delighteth did her feet tread as she crossed the doorstep of her father's house that morning. A large company of relatives and her exasperated parents were waiting for her in the courtyard. "Thou hast disgraced me before all these people!" she heard her father say in a loud and terrible voice. "Shame upon thee! *Chee!* Thou art a scorn and a derision!" And he plucked off his sandal and for the first time in his life struck his little daughter and spat in her face.

There came a day, a memorable day, when Star read from the prophet Isaiah, *"I hid not My face from shame and spitting."* She was overwhelmed when she read those words, for she knew herself to be unworthy of the honor that was set upon her when she was allowed in that one small but painful way to follow in His steps. But this was out of her sight then, and as she wiped her face, sick at heart and ashamed, she began to despair. "There is no hope for me, no hope at all for me. I am a bird shut up in an iron cage."

Thus things were; nothing could make her happy. All the time she was thinking: "What can I do so that I may be a Christian?" But instead of finding any way, she was every day more and more closely watched and rigorously dealt with, for her parents were determined to crush her desire, and they tried to force her to rub Siva's ashes on her forehead, which she continued to refuse to do. Then her mother was sure that either her ammal had given her a magic medicine which had destroyed her mind, or that she was possessed by a demon. And the little Mimosa, Star's younger sister, looked on with grave and disapproving eyes and saw nothing but that her sister had disgraced the family; and this she knew was a dreadful shame to them all.

Those days must indeed have been dolorous. Her Gospel of St. Mark was taken from her. She had not had the chance to read it, but she had found help and comfort in the "feel of it" folded in her sari. To touch the small flimsy pages and stiff cardboard back was fortifying; now she must do without that. If it were proved that she was possessed there would be much beating and wailing and chasing about to force the spirit to go elsewhere. But of all this she hardly dared to think.

"With the pen of love, with the water of tears, and on paper of suffering," the little lover wrote to her Beloved. And the answer came back to the little lover, as it did to the great lover of long ago, in words of comforting.

15

What Great Conflict

MEANWHILE we waited, hearing nothing of this, hearing only the heart-breaking word, "She has given up everything. She has rubbed ashes on her forehead." But we knew that if she had denied her Savior it could only have been the denial of the lips, wrung from her by great misery. And what had she endured before she had yielded? We thought of Peter and of how humbly thankful he must be because of the way his Lord has turned his very fall to the help of others. It was a relief to remember that Star knew about Peter.

She had been nearly a month at home when "truth without even the measure of a rapeseed of lie in it" reached us, or so we were assured it was. "Does not the scorpion, offended, sting and go on stinging?" How could so young a girl hold out against that? She had been utterly subdued. We drew together then, we who cared most, and we prayed.

Then a small voice within said softly, but terribly distinctly: "What of him that heareth the word and anon with joy receiveth it; yet hath he not root in himself, but dureth for a while; for when tribulation or persecution ariseth because of the word, by-and-by he is offended?" Satan can quote Scripture with ravaging effect.

"Lord, answer him for me."

If this book finds its way to any of the harder battlefields of the earth, whether at home or overseas, it will certainly find some who know the torment of this penetrating whisper. The soul can be racked by it. Worse, it can be weakened. But let that soul gather itself up as the wave gathers itself up before it curls over; let it fall even as the wave falls and is shattered on the shore; then, broken at the feet of its Lord—nothing kept back, not even its fears—it will be empowered for a new gathering up of spiritual energies, a new pouring forth. There are psalms that are such waves of prayer gathered up, poured forth. They are born of the depths of tremendous experiences. And he who is called to do more than play with life thanks God for those psalms.

In the silence which filled the first minutes of that hour we remembered the years of the right hand of the Most High: The floods stood upright as an heap. The walls (of Jericho) fell down flat. The sun stood still and the moon stayed. The iron did swim. The Lord opened the eyes of the young man, and he saw; and, behold, the mountain was full of horses and chariots of fire round about Elisha.

Our story belongs to a time before this wonderful day of the spade and the pickaxe. But those who had the happiness of being sure that the jewel of spiritual revelation is set in the pure gold of truth, not in the mixed metal of myth and legend, had no need to wait for proofs before they could enjoy the comfort of the Scriptures. And so we, who belong to that company, rose from our knees enlightened, strengthened and relieved.

But five days passed and still we heard nothing but devastating rumors; those five days were like five months. And yet I can imagine the question, "Why such piercing anguish about a child who was safe in her own home, not in a den of iniquity?" Perhaps the question is inevitable if the reader has absorbed the thought that what St. John calls the darkness is merely a lesser light. Many books now say that it is so; but to read the New Testament is to breathe a different air.

Then news came that was not rumor; the date of Star's marriage was fixed. "Women received their dead raised to life again; and others were tortured, not accepting deliverance." But we could wait no longer without knowing more. We took the risk and sent a messenger to her father to ask him if she might come to see us again, even if she might not stay. If only we could comfort her and fortify her for what would be a long-protracted martyrdom, it would be something. And what if our God had already commanded deliverance? God is unto us a God of deliverances. Perhaps the first half of that verse in Hebrews was for us; *but we must be willing for the second half.*

It was a conflict. "I would that ye knew what great conflict."

And yet, could we have seen her as the spiritual watchers saw her, we should have sung for joy that day, for they saw life, life triumphant. The silver birch in the wind on the bare hillside under the cloudy sky is not giving way. Rooted, invisibly sustained, it is never done to death. Wind-swept; it stands there; it is not overcome.

16

A Token for Good

STAR was not at home, nor was her father, when the messenger arrived. Her mother invited him in, and he told her his errand. A child playing nearby, hearing the talk of the grown-up people, understood that this was Star's matter and ran off, bursting with her news, to find her. Having found her, "Your ammal has sent a messenger to ask your parents to let you come back and learn," she said.

Star was thrilled. "Where is he?"

The messenger recalling old days as he looks at Star, wondering at the way young things grow up.

"He has gone, but he is to return in the evening for your father's answer. When your mother saw him she told him that you were either possessed by an evil spirit or else pining for your ammal, who had given magical medicine to you and bewitched you. She said that if you were not allowed to go back to her you would probably die; but that your father, who was out, would not consent to let you go, and she told him to return in the evening and talk to your father."

This was amazing news. Star rejoiced exceedingly, and her faith and hope returned. Her mother told her nothing, and she did not tell her mother anything of this that she had heard. (A child can be very wise.)

The evening came at last, and the messenger came back to talk to her father. She was in the room when he came; she was praying in her heart, and all her words were these: "O living God, change my father's heart that he may let me go."

When her father saw the messenger he was very angry.

"Why didst thou come?"

"The ammal sent me to ask if you will allow your daughter to learn with her," said the messenger.

"What has she to do with my daughter? Does she think I am a poor man and cannot look after my own child? If the Supreme gave me fifty children I have the means to look after them all. Only the poor send their children to Christians to be educated."

"Not so, not so," said the messenger soothingly; "it is only that she loves your child and wants to see her."

For long they talked together. At last her father said: "No one can change my mind and will. I have no intention of letting my daughter go; no one on earth can change my will."

At this point her mother interposed. "Do not let her go to learn, but let her go and see the ammal. Perhaps after seeing her she will be happier and forget her infatuation."

Then her father began to yield: "Yes, that ammal has undoubtedly given the child magical medicine, and she cannot rest till she sees her again." To the messenger he said: "Take her, but bring her back at once." "I will faithfully bring her back the day after tomorrow," said the messenger.

"When I heard this," wrote Star in her notebook, "my burden fell off, for I felt sure that if for one hour only my father let me go, God would work for me and deliver me entirely. So I praised God, and with my praises mixed prayers that my father's mind might not be changed before the morning. In the early dawn the messenger came for me.

"As we walked the seven miles that lay between my home and the bungalow the messenger instructed me in what he thought was the proper behavior of a child in a bungalow. He advised me to keep strict bounds upon myself and not to show my real heart. I answered him nothing, but I felt: 'This is all impossible talk; I have already lost my heart to my amma. How, then, can I set strict bounds to my heart?'"

And in this she thought according to the nature of her people, in whom is such a fidelity in love that whoso has experienced it learns to count upon it; I at least have never found it fail. Once the love of the heart has fastened on another—however unworthy that other may be—it continues fastened: it never works loose. Often I think that it must be more than a dear reflection; it belongs to the very nature of the Love that, having loved, loves its own unto the end.

And while those two walked across the plain that Sunday morning, I, sitting in my room thinking of Star, only of Star, read in the Psalms for the strengthening of faith. Many verses had a voice, and that voice was hers. "I am so fast in prison that I cannot get out. Comfort the soul of Thy servant: for unto Thee, O Lord, do I lift up my soul. In the time of my trouble I will call upon Thee, for Thou hearest me. Among the gods there is none like unto Thee, O Lord; there is not one that can do as Thou doest. Teach me Thy way, O Lord, and I will walk in Thy truth. Oh, knit my heart unto Thee." And then my own longing found voice in the cry—hardly could it be called a prayer, for faith was tired that day—"Show some token upon me for good." Oh, what a token for good it would be if Star might come back to me.

The quiet minutes passed. The bell began to ring, and I was just about to get ready for church when there was a little sound at the door; a little hand pushed the sunblind back, and I had my child again.

The Tamil language is like a flowery field full of lovewords and joy-words and pictures that show happiness. The delighted heart is as the lotus that has seen the sun; the one who has been given an unexpected pleasure is as one who has had a glimpse into the Unseen; and among the words of joy is one which shows the speechless rapture of a soul ravished, swept as by a wind of delight far away out of itself. But the faint pencil of the notebook turns to a Bible story for help to show that shining minute. "When we came to the bungalow, I forgot all about the messenger's warning words. It was as though Jacob had received his lost Jos. I fell on my amma's neck and we wept for joy together."

That minute, and all the minutes round about it, are like little grains of jasper or any sparkling dust of gems one can imagine. They sparkle now as I look back a long time afterwards. To Star they were as stars.

Suddenly, as she stood beside me, her arms round me and mine round her, she swayed and would have fallen. I laid her on the mat, and on that mat she lay for full four weeks. It did indeed look like the work of the adversary ("Go to the Christians and die," say the Hindus), and so it appeared to Star.

17

All Night Long the Lizards Cheeped

"ALL night long the lizards cheeped." This is a word from the notebook, for Star heard them and thought that the god whom she had forsaken had sent the lizards to show these signs of ill-omen. "Let it be so," she said to herself. "Though my reason should forsake me, still it is worthwhile; though I should die, still it is worthwhile." But of this she said nothing to me that night, and all we saw was a child who lay in deep fatigue and in silence hour after hour till our hearts failed us for fear. "Go to the Christians and die."

And now a great difficulty was suddenly thrust upon us. We had to nurse a caste child through a serious illness without breaking caste. To have done anything which her parents would have felt polluting, such as to let one of our kind servants touch anything she had to eat or drink, would have greatly disturbed her people, and they would probably have carried her off at once, even at the risk of her life, rather than allow that to continue. Fortunately I had a new lunch-basket furnished with electro-plated saucepan and so on, which had never been used, and we had milk milked into this saucepan and heated it on a spirit stove, far from the kitchen. Another mercy was that her illness was the kind of dysentery which allows a milk diet. We had no doctor to tell us so. But at such times help comes. Things are never too difficult.

Our chief anxiety, of course, was her father. We sent to tell him that she was ill, but, as she puts it, "the messenger being a kind but not a truthful man, deceived my father with various stories till at last he came for me himself. He came in wrath, but he went away in love. He saw me as I used to be, full of happiness and loving him, and he found that my amma had nursed me without once breaking my caste, and that she was in all ways careful to observe his wishes. This exceedingly astonished him, and he agreed to let me stay for another week."

During that week Star's grandmother came to the house, and seeing a picture of Daniel in the lions' den she demanded the story. She was a dauntless old lady, and after hearing of his valor she greatly respected Daniel, who was, she considered, "not the kind of Guru who dare not climb a cottage roof to scare a fowl and yet professed to open heaven to the believer," and this was to his credit and to the credit of his religion; but nothing anyone could say seemed to make much impression upon her. "Are there not many roads leading to a village? By your way you go to attain Release, by my way I shall attain." There was neither salt, nor tamarind, nor juice in our words, she said, and our stories had neither head nor tail, always excepting Daniel's.

The week was allowed to spin out into a month, and other relatives came to see Star; among them, on a day that has a little crown on it (we did not see the crown at the time), Star's father brought her younger sister—the little beloved Mimosa. But that was an anxious hour, for the father, provoked by the younger girl's earnest wish to hear more, seemed about to command Star's return. Such days were days of tension and much prayer, but "I am the Ground of thy beseeching" is a truth that nothing can assail.

And all through those first wrestlings with the enemy and first gladness in the triumph of our Lord, and on through the years that followed till he was taken from us, stood Walker Iyer, faithful in strength, and his gentle, loving wife, with whom everything was shared. Often as I look at the joy the later years have brought, the joy of the larger family and the Fellowship of

Gold Cord, I wonder if ever it would have been mine if it had not been for their friendship and comradeship. Their works do follow them.

18

A Misread Word

AFTER her illness and recovery, Star's father had not the heart to force her to return home when she so ardently desired to stay within reach of us and be taught more. So he allowed her to continue to live with her uncle and come to us for teaching. But we were often in camp. And when I had to leave her behind, as I had to do then, I felt like the kine whose calves were shut up at home, and who, though they took the straight way to the place appointed, went along the highway, lowing as they went.

The Bible prayers were my stronghold then: Show Thy marvelous lovingkindness, O Thou that savest by Thy right hand them which put their trust in Thee from those that rise up against them. Keep her as the apple of the eye, hide her under the shadow of Thy wings.

Once when we were far away in camp, Star's parents heard of it, and thinking that all had been providentially arranged so that the child could be retrieved without any agitating scenes with the white people, her father determined to effect this, and full of his purpose, he went to his brother-in-law's house expecting to find her there. But she had gone to the bungalow for her daily lesson with Pearl, whom we had left behind to teach her. So he sent his servant to fetch her.

"Thy father has come; he is waiting at thy uncle's house. He wants thee to come at once," he said.

"Then my heart was frightened"—thus the notebook. "Another dark time is upon me, I thought. I had no faith. I was not ready to go with the servant. 'Go; I will come in a few minutes,' I said to him, and he returned to my father.

"Then I went to my amma's bathroom and shut the door and said to God, 'Now my father has come to take me away. There is no one to talk to him, there is no one to help me but You alone. If Iyer and Amma were here, even they could not help me if my father were set on taking me away. But You can help me. So please give me a promise that my father will not take me away, but that I shall return to the bungalow.'

"Then I waited, I thought there must be a voice from God. But all was quiet. Still I waited, and suddenly the trouble was lifted from my heart and peace came upon me. Then I thought I heard a word that said, *'Read Malachi 4:2.'* I had never read that book, nor could I at that time read properly, and I misread a word as I spelled out the verse. Instead of reading 'Ye shall go forth and grow up as calves of the stall,' I read 'Ye shall go forth and come back as calves of the stall,' for my eyes were excited and I overlooked one letter which changed the sense."

By this time nearly an hour had passed. The servant came for her again. "If thou dost not hasten, thy father will carry thee straight off home," he said. "He is very angry with thee." But she was ready. Tranquilly then she walked down the sandy path where she had found the copper coin on that unforgotten Sunday, saying to herself (unawares anticipating what a later day gave her in the Revised Version), "I will come back, I will return gambolling like a calf." For the word that she had read (or mis-read) was an oracle of truth to her. She never for a moment questioned or doubted its bearing on her own case, desperate as that seemed at the moment. "There was all but a rainbow round the words he wrote," is the way the second in command of a Frontier Force described the writing of his Commanding Officer. So did Star feel that day about those words of the prophet Malachi. There was all but a rainbow round them.

When she reached her father his face was like thunder, but she was not frightened. She ran to him and kissed him, and asked him why he had come. "I cannot tell thee now," he said, "for if I begin to talk to thee my heart will melt." Then she told him that she was not afraid because of the word that her God had given to her. "I shall return," she assured him, "gambolling like a calf." He listened half stunned, "My arm is weak, I cannot do anything against thy God and thy ammal's God!"—the words seemed to be forced from him. And he stretched out his arm as though to seize her, but dropped it by his side. Then he told Star to read to him from her Book, and she read to him from Acts 9, about Saul going to kill the Lord's people and how the Lord met him on the way. And she told him that he was like Saul. He had not come to kill her body but he had come to kill her faith, and the Lord had met him and stopped him. Then her father asked her to pray for him, and after she had prayed he said that he would never take her away unless she wanted to go, for he feared the Supreme God. "But I knew," is her frank comment, "that as he was a Hindu he would not find it possible to keep his promise. I knew that he would come again, but I was sure that God would protect me whatever happened, as He had protected me this time. From that day forth I was at rest, and knew that I should not be 'a heathen forever.' That prayer about my marriage was answered."

How well I remember the camp from which we returned to meet this sweet delight. It had been difficult to give one's whole strength to the work in the villages because there was always the thought of Star behind everything. I was still lowing as I went. It would have been faithless to remain at home, and the trusty Pearl was with her, but mother-feelings listen to no reason. They go on lowing.

And imagination painted all sorts of possible perils. What if her father came? There was just one word that held me from hastening back to her: "Thou wilt keep him in perfect peace whose mind (imagination) is stayed on Thee, because he trusteth in Thee."

Once in a young and careless hour I had painted that verse for a friend without looking it up, and wrote *trusted* instead of *trusteth.* It was framed and glazed and hung on the wall—a spray of pink honeysuckle wandered across one corner, in the way flowers did wander about texts in those days, and it looked quite nice—till someone read it, and turned with a quick, "That's wrong! It's better than that." I thought of that then. And a verse we had written in large Tamil script, and hung across the mud wall of a little prayer room, where the pastor had asked us to take the meetings for the Christians of the place, helped me very much. "I will cry unto God most High; unto God that performeth all things for me"—in Tamil, *"God who is going to finish all for me."* I read that verse over and over again during the long preaching. How can any, we often wonder, bear up through the fears and the desolations of life without rock underfoot? Not to be sure of whom we have believed, or of what we have believed, must be like standing on quicksand with a blinding scurry of mist about one, and no clear air overhead.

From that camp we returned to find our child so happy that she really did resemble her gambolling calves. Then after the jubilant welcome we heard the dear little story of protection; but the near and tender touch of a love which can turn a misread word to blessed profit did not seem a little thing to us that day.

19

Violets by the Roadside

AFTER a while we were allowed to take Star with us when we were out in camp (I forget with what restrictions about food). The freshness of dew is on those memories, though anything less like dew than the blistering heat, when there are no large trees, and the tents have to be pitched under palmyra palms on blazing sand, can hardly be imagined. When it was cool it was also wet, so that camp generally meant the dry season and heat. But nothing mattered. We were strong with the joy of morning.

And we had need to be, for our journeys were not luxurious. They were wholly delightful, however, especially to Star. What could have been more enjoyable than the start, in a long comical procession of bullock bandies, each one packed inside with people, and festooned outside with all manner of things? Pots and pans and buckets, a kettle or two, bundles of firewood, bulgy sacks of oddments that had not gone in the baggage-cart, were roped to the sides of the curved mat roof and made a cheerful clatter. Each bandy had a heap of straw piled on the top of the roof or slung in a net underneath, where also was hung an earthen cruse of water and probably a basketful of fowls. Their cackle mixed with the general racket, the jingle of the bullock bells, and the shouts of the drivers made a most exciting noise. Just as we were about to start a bandy driver would melt into the dusk—he had not yet had his curry and rice, a fellow carter would kindly explain; or we would discover that one of the bandies had forgotten its lantern, and the whole procession would be held up while that lantern was retrieved and tied to the bandy or swung to the pole just out of reach of the bullocks' tails. It was hot inside the bandies and unbelievably stuffy, for the bare and glistening brown back of the driver filled up most of the open end in front, and, in our cart at least, there were always three, which meant that if one of us wanted to turn all must turn; but it was pure bliss.

Camp had its merry times, for Star had a scandalous habit of playing pranks on the somewhat sober-minded older women of the band. One day we returned from work to be met outside my tent by growls, snarls, barks, scuffling. "Dogs! Chet!" I can see their good brown faces winkled up in amazement as, with uplifted hands they gasped, "But no dogs be!" till a paroxysm of yelps suddenly tailed off into laughter, and a dishevelled Star wriggled out from under the low camp cot in the corner.

Long afterwards, when our Fellowship had come into being and we had the gayest of doctors, nurses, teachers, and all manner of people ready for any manner of service, who had been gathered from eight or nine different countries, but were one in earnest purpose and in happiness of heart, we added a verse to one of our litanies of thanksgiving:

> God of the sparkle on our day,
>   Gift of the Sun;
> Laughter that lifts; all lovely, gay,
>   Ripples of fun.
> God of the little things,
>   We adore Thee,
>   Come before Thee,
> Grateful in loving thanksgiving.

Star was all eagerness over other things too. I can see the bullock cart drawn up near the door of the tent (the end paper shows one of us there with an old dame); the bulls loosely tethered, munching straw steadily; a knot of small girls and their attendant babies round the yoke-and-pole end; and perched on the pole, Star, "preaching."

Her small hearers were listening spellbound. I wondered what she was saying, something interesting, certainly. She had a way of her own of saying things. Once she happened to be alone on the verandah at night, with a lamp set behind her, so that it cast a small circle of light round her as she sat on the floor. When I asked her how long she had been alone she answered gravely: "I have not been alone. There are five here; God the Father, God the Son, and God the Holy Spirit, the devil, and me. But the devil," she added with great calmness, "is outside there," pointing to the darkness beyond the circle of lamplight.

And we had heavenly times when we loved our Lord Jesus together. Is it not true that among the dearest hours of life are the hours when we meet like that, soul to soul, with no fear at all of being misunderstood, no fear at all of chill? Hours when, with another dearly loved and absolutely trusted, we press on, and "little whispers from the spiritual world" come through.

That lovely word is from Wilson of the Antarctic, Scott's companion in his last terrific journey to the Land of Everlasting Joy: "A happy life is not built up of tours abroad and pleasant holidays, but of little clumps of violets by the roadside, hidden away almost, so that only those can see them who have God's peace and love in their hearts; in one long continuous chain of little joys; little whispers from the spiritual world; little gleams of sunshine on our daily work." But who can tell of these things? All who know our Lord Jesus, know what He does for the least of His followers when He draws near and refreshes them with the light of His Presence. What will it be when no shadow of interruption shall ever cross that light? "When shall I at full gather myself in Thee, that for Thy love I feel not myself, but Thee only, above all feeling and all manner?" And yet, far from this though I be, Lord, Thou knowest all things: Thou knowest that I love Thee: Thou, O Lord, art the Thing that I long for:

> One thing have I desired, my God, of Thee,
> That will I seek—Thy house be home to me.
>
> I would not breathe an alien, other air;
> I would be with Thee, O Thou fairest Fair.
>
> For I would see the beauty of my Lord,
> And hear Him speak, who is my heart's Adored.
>
> O Love of loves, and can such wonder dwell
> In Thy great Name of names, Immanuel?
>
> Thou with Thy child, Thy child at home with Thee,
> O Love of loves, I love, I worship Thee.

Such an hour leaves the heart close to His lovers everywhere, gathering violets with them by the roadside. For truly fellow lovers are near to one another; years make no distance, nor country, nor climate, nor color. This kind of loving laughs at all dividing things.

20

They Might have Belonged to the Same Clan

ONE day we went to the Fort; this time we were not turned back. Unhindered, we wandered through tiny, silent streets, so strangely silent that they seemed like streets in a city of the dead. The houses were solidly built of stone and brick, with heavily barred windows; one house was three-storied, colored buff, terra-cotta and blue. Its fine wood carving on the lower verandah, and a pineapple decoration on the upper, gave it a nice air of distinction. We walked on down a short street; it had four small quaint houses on either side, but they all turned blind eyes to the street. We sat down on one of the little stone verandahs facing an iron-clamped door, and wondered which door would open. The stillness was oppressive. Was the place asleep or dead?

At last the door opposite opened, and a woman looked out. She was going to slam it, dismayed, when a smile reassured her, and before she could make up her mind what to do, we were on the other side of the street, persuading her to let us sit on her verandah, and to keep her door open, so that we could talk with her, we outside, she inside. We sat so for an hour or more; her dark eyes looked deep into ours, and stirred our hearts with strong desire that she should understand. And after we had gone away that woman's face came back to me. I felt as though I had seen her before.

Next time we were in that region I went again, taking Star, who was never so happy as when we were out doing such work together. On the far side of the enclosure we found a grey old temple within a high red and white wall. A tamarind tree grew beside it, and glad to get out of the brilliant light—light beating down from unclouded blue, and light beating up from the glittering sand—we stood in the cool, green shade and prayed for an opportunity to give our happy message.

Soon from the distance voices jangled through the universal silence. Then some field women strolled across the open and called to us in the friendliest way. They were the Fort people's servants, they said; they worked in the Fort fields outside, and did the rough work of the place. They thought us wise for not knocking at the doors. "It would have disturbed the women. Why should you trouble them?"

"The evangelization of the world in this generation" is an inspiring motto; but how are you to evangelize people when you cannot get at them? The field women had work to do, and they left us under the tree.

We had not knocked at any door, partly lest we should frighten the shy inhabitants, and partly because we wanted to be led to the heart prepared. So once more we walked past the shut-up houses, looking for an open door, and, finding one, we had a talk with the girl who called us in. Again I had that curious sense of having seen her somewhere before.

She was a young wife, tall and slim, with hair that waved and curled round a smooth low brow, and eyes that shone when she spoke to us or smiled, but when she was only listening the light passed; her normal expression was wistful. She sighed while Star told her of the God who had sent us to tell her He loved her. "Who loves me?" she interrupted. "I have no children."

We knew enough of the customs of the Fort to understand. We had heard a smothered cry as we passed the house where a widow lived, in what a child called the eighth (very innermost) room of the house. Only a thread, her husband's life, held that fate from this girl. The fate of a young, childless widow is very hard.

As the two girls looked at each other after that sorrowful interruption, I noticed a strange resemblance. There was the same little tilt of the head and quick appraising glance of the eye. They belonged to the same caste, but they might have belonged to the same clan—fantastic thought. Then Star, leaning forward, held out her hands beseechingly, "This news was beautiful to me and the joy of joys," and the other, leaning back, lest defiling Christian hands should touch her, answered only with a yawn. "Is that so?" she said at last, and rose; "I must go and do my cooking."

Had she the heart prepared? It did not seem like that. And yet one never knows. The seed strikes roots sometimes in a narrow crevice in the rock.

We found another door open, and went in full of expectation, to find a mother and her pretty children. The room was dark except for the shaft of light which fell from the open door, for the barred window was shuttered. A tall brass lampstand hung with oleander flowers stood on the floor, and in the corner there was a bed of rosewood finely carved and used as a seat. A pile of silk caries lay on it, crimson, orange, golden-brown; the shaft of sunlight fell on the heaped-up color. There was color too in the group on the floor where, half in light and half in shadow, making unconscious pictures, the mother and children sat and looked at us with that calm scrutiny which in India precedes speech, be the speech when it comes never so trivial. "Why have you got no jewels and no oil on your hair?" they asked at length, and we launched into conversation.

And one by one the women from the inner room came out. There was not a sound or a movement as we spoke to them. And we longed to stay with those so curiously familiar-faced women (why were they so familiar?), become Fort women to them, and tell them about the love of our Savior over and over, till we could be sure that they understood. A man saw us as we left the house, but he took no notice; so far as getting in was concerned, the sad little place was open at last. Any woman could go in now.

21

Nearer Still than its Nest

I HAD often wondered how it was that this child, who had never heard before, was so ready to understand. We were to see that miracle of miracles, an immediate response to the call of the unseen Spring, more than once through those years, but not often enough to dim the bright sense of wonder. For it is always wonderful to stand with the happy angels and watch a soul take color, like a dewdrop in sunrise.

We were in camp when I heard for the first time some of the things that I have written in this story. Our tents were pitched on an expanse of white sand, far inland, but it reminded us of the sea. The day had been hot, and all day long people had been coming from the village near, not to listen, but to stare and talk about nothing. Our crowded tents had been stifling. The noisy day had left us tired. "Come," I said to Star, who was with us, "let us go out and cool." Only the shadow of some stunted palms crossed the whiteness of the sand. Only the rustle of their leaves broke the silence. We lay down in a pool of moonlight and looked at the long silver ribs and ripples where the wind had played with the sand. "Authentic tidings of invisible things," to whom do they not come on such a night? The holy beauty of moonlight in India is such that the heart is carried away to the moonlit garden where, very early in the morning, the women came bringing the spices which they had prepared, and found the Lord of Life had risen.

After Calvary, after that strange visit to the spirits in prison, did our dear Lord find (as we so often do) thoughts of peace in the pure moonlight? That same holy peace, that air of purity was about us then.

"Amma," whispered Star, at last, so gently that it might have been the wind speaking softly, "this reminds me of the first night I spoke with God." "Tell me about it," I said; and she told me.

And after she had told me we were quiet for a while. I was thinking of the wonder of that "nearer still than its nest," the unknown, the unfamiliar, nearer than anything known and familiar could be.

For ah, the Master is so fair,
　　His smile so sweet to banished men,
That they who see Him unaware
　　Can never rest on earth again.
And they who see Him risen afar
　　On God's right hand to welcome them,
Forgetful stand of home and land
　　Desiring fair Jerusalem.

Dreamily the words drifted through me, but they did not explain the call of the Spring in the heart of this little bird. I left it. It could not be understood; it could only be accepted with thanksgiving. And yet how sweet and simple it was: "The soul breaks away to its own, with the natural flight of a bird from its Autumn nest, at the call of an unseen Spring, to the far-off land that is nearer still than its nest, because it is in its heart." This little bird had flown like that, and she had flown quite alone. I am told by one, wise in the way of birds, that young birds do fly alone. The old birds do not show them the way to the land across the sea. How do they find it, then? How did the bird of this story find the land of her heart's desire? God help us to reckon with a more courageous confidence on the infinite power of Love to direct the flight of His birds.

For the call does not come from nowhere. It is the pledge to the bird that across the sea lies the Summer (for if there were no Summer, there would be no call); and it flies in a sure faith. This is the mystery of the call of Christ to the human soul, even though it be only the soul of a child.

"What helped thee most through those weeks when they took thee away from us?" I asked her. She knew so little of the Bible then that I wondered what she would say. She told me how she had kept the Gospel of St. Mark tied up in her sari as long as she could, and after it was discovered and taken from her, she had remembered that no one could take away her Savior: "Who shall separate us from the love of Christ?" She clung to those words which are among the first we teach to one like Star. And the burning fiery furnace story had encouraged her. For if He walked in that fire, then she knew that He could walk in any fire. "But what a good thing it was that the ropes were burned, for if they had not been the three men could not have walked with Him," she added meditatively.

There is a power that is not of earth about these stories. For searching or for strengthening they find the soul just where it is, and do their mighty work. They are far more than stories, just as the words of our Scripture are far more than words. That is why we do at times find something, perhaps quite simple and familiar, shine forth as though illuminated in gold and precious colors. For so are we given, by the mercy of the Lord, grace to help in time of need.

Never let us fear for our beloved. After long rain, when there is no moon and the stars are blanketed by heavy clouds, we have often seen the low rice fields, the runlet by the roadside, the trees that border the road, jewelled and sparkling. It is indeed as though the sky above us had poured her stars upon the earth, sown them like seeds of light. The rice field is not a cloth of gold, but a carpet of moving jewels; the runlet is a spangled scarf; the tree is a Christmas tree with all its stars alive. And nothing of this is seen till it is dark.

Fear thou not the cloudy evening.
  By dim waters fireflies glisten,
'Mid the dark leaves of the tree
  Starry hosts are moving; listen,
Listen, for they speak to thee:
My Lord will take care of me.
Fear thou not the moonless darkness.
  Moonless nights discover fireflies,
Star-seeds of eternity,
  Luminous when common day dies.
Words of light are sown for thee:
My Lord will take care of me.

O God, my Savior, overlook me not. The Lord will take care of me. These two little seeds of light (from the Septuagint rendering of Psalm 27:9 and Psalm 40:17) can be fireflies of living joy to the troubled heart. My Lord will take care of me, He will take care of them—He will take care of *him*, of *her*. He will not overlook the little beloved one who is out in the dark weather.

22

The Coming of Supu

IT was about this time that we became aware of a stirring in Uncrowned-King. It was entirely among the young. A boy, Star's cousin, believed and made up his mind to be a Christian. In his father's house there was an upper room, the roof of which was supported on short, round, whitewashed pillars. The room, seen as I saw it, in the blaze of noon, leaves an impression of glare: glaring sky looking in, glaring white pillars, the roofs of the town glaring red. Into this glaring room the father led his son, tied him with a rope to one of the pillars, and spoke a few fearful words. The punishment, if he persisted in this folly, would be cayenne pepper rubbed into his eyes. (I have seen a boy blinded by that torture.) But the boy did not flinch. He was kept for five days tied to the pillar, and then it was the father, not the boy, who gave in. Later both he and Star's younger brother, whose name means "Very dear," became Christians. And there was another; but to tell of him I must go back a little.

Star's home was one of two houses belonging to her father and his brother, both opening on the same courtyard. Among the cousins in the second house was a boy called Supu, a few years older than Star, and her great friend. Star could not see in the twilight, and Supu was always at hand to help her.

If she happened to be out of doors after sunset he would never rest till he had found her, and then he would take her in his arms and carry her home. He told her that when he grew up he would ask for her, and she promised to be his little bride. But Supu was left-handed.

One day, when Star was eight years old, her mother gave her a new sari, and as she put it on both parents made much of her. She noticed her dear Supu looking very sorrowful, and as soon as he could see her alone he told her that because he was left-handed her parents had decided to give her to somebody else, though according to custom he was a suitable bridegroom. The putting on of the new sari was the first ceremony of betrothal. Star was distressed and told Supu that when she was grown up she would refuse that other, not knowing that in such a matter she would be helpless in the strong hands of her parents.

This boy had been one of a group of lads and men who stood near the well that evening when we thought nothing had been done, that evening when Star first heard of the living God. And he, too, received the word into his heart, but he was silent even to Star. Perhaps he was not sure enough to speak. He was not ready to plunge his family into grief on his account, and to confess himself a believer would mean that. So Supu said nothing.

And then we went out again, going from town to town and village to village. Supu came to one of these preachings again, and he could not hesitate longer:

> Love so amazing, so divine,
> Demands my soul, my life, my all

Demands? But that is not enough. He turned it to a word of decision, "*Shall have* my soul, my life, my all"; and he faced the cost, the terrible cost: there was no place for a Christian in his father's home. Star knew nothing of this, nor did we.

The day he came is marked by a scar. For us who work in India there is no quick martyrdom. And yet no one who goes out in the battlefield and fights our Lord's enemies is for long without a wound, the kind of wound that heals slowly and leaves a scar. But we have a cactus here which shoots forth a white flower something like a many petalled lily. Straight from a stem that is all stabbing thorn that flower springs. Sometimes there are twenty or thirty on a single tall stem: the thorny day bears many flowers. My flower that day was the coming of Supu. He arrived at the Great-Lake bungalow a few minutes before I returned from a village called Red-Goddess, a place dominated by Star's caste folk, and therefore embittered. I had been defeated there and was sorrowful. The rulers of this present darkness do indeed put forth strength when they see a soul, born in their shadow, all but translated into the kingdom of light. They had dragged that soul back, and "thorny" seems too slight a word for the piercing of that day. By the time I returned from Red-Goddess the late meal we call breakfast in South India was on the table, and I saw a new face—Supu's.

Star was living again with her uncle then, and coming to us for lessons. She joined us after breakfast at prayers; she did not know yet of Supu's arrival.

When the breakfast things were cleared away she came in as usual, and we all sat down on the floor together, the Iyer and his wife, the Indian sisters of the itinerating band, Star and I, and the servants who were our friends. The custom was for the chapter to be read round, verse by verse—a distracting way of reading, but to the Tamil enjoyable. Star was busy finding the place and probably glancing down the column of fine Tamil to make sure of any hard words—for to read aloud when you are near your beginnings can be an ordeal—and so she did not notice her cousin who was sitting on the far side of the Iyer. He came last in the circle, and when he read his verse Star almost dropped her Bible in astonishment. She wanted to get up and dance. She could not attend to the reading. She was too glad to read or to listen. After prayers she asked the Iyer why he had not told her that her cousin had come. He had wanted to see her face, he said, when she had that beautiful surprise.

23

Star and Supu

WITHIN an hour or two that quiet room where we had read together was filled with storm. Crowds of Supu's relatives came and battered him with words. They brought a professional orator, whose flow was like a river in full spate. When this torrent of argument and abuse left Supu unmoved, the orator suddenly changed his tactics, and we had a weird half-hour of what appeared to be hypnotic suggestion, far more trying than the torrent to the Indian mind. This failing, there remained only the last and hardest to withstand. "Thy mother, she who bore thee, is she to die of a broken heart? O destroyer of thy mother, hast thou no filial feeling, no love, no shame?" This was almost too much, and we who shared it were torn with Supu then. At last he cried: "You will not let me follow my Lord; I cannot give Him up; He died for me." Then they scourged him with the scourge of the tongue. And they went away, each man beating his breast in an abandon of dismay, disgust, and horror. "He has fallen into the pit!"

Star knew exactly the other thing that they would say: "I felt that it would not be at all for the glory of God to have such things said; so though we loved each other far more than ever, we promised each other that we would not think of marrying, but serve God faithfully all the days of our lives, so that no one could throw dust at the name of our holy God and say that Supu had become a Christian just to win me.

"One night our grandmother, who was keeping house for our uncle, came to see us. She said to Supu: 'Oh, thou art a clever fellow and a wily; I know what is in thy heart!' Supu tried hard to make her believe that truly he had come only for the love of the Lord who had drawn him. She would not listen. I was very indignant about it, but she would not listen to me either. She sent a message to his father, and he came and talked vehemently to Supu, and struck him for disgracing himself by following me after my father had refused me to him. It seemed to him most ignoble and his wrath burned. Supu bore it bravely, but some time afterwards he said to me: 'It is said that no man can live without a wife. Promise me that by and by thou wilt be my wife.' Then I was more angry than I ever had been in all my life before. I said: 'If you came out of Hinduism for my sake, you had better go back into it. If your motive is not pure, you had better be a Hindu.'

"'But when I came out I had no such motive,' said poor Supu. It is only that now, when I listen to the talk of the Christians about me, I hear this word constantly sounded in my ears.' But I answered him: 'If you are going to listen to the talk of the Christians, you will be as they are; you had better then find a bride among them, and be in all ways like them.' I said this being young and not understanding these things fully, but only knowing that I did not want my dear Supu to resemble the Christians we saw about us.[2] And I told him that I wanted to live quite a different kind of life.

"'Then let us give up the thought,' he said; 'only let us always love each other.' And I agreed, and kneeling down in the sand by the thorn bushes, near where my living God had caused me to find the copper coin, I prayed for him in these words: 'Lord, open his eyes to see what You will do with his life if only he will be strong and not lean to the words of men.' And he, too, with tears prayed for strength."

So it was that these two young lovers gave themselves to be made like those soldiers of King David who were "prepared for the war." They did not fully understand what they had done, for they had hardly learned the meaning of our word "discipline"—a word not easily translated into Tamil; but their hearts had chosen the thing itself, and they feared compromise, they feared weakness. If this were indeed the way to the utmost that Love could ask of them, could Love ask too much? They were willing; they were eager to follow; even though it must mean for them both, death to the natural.

They had by this time read the great words in St. John: "Verily, verily, I say unto you, Except a corn of wheat fall into the ground and die, it abideth alone; but if it die it bringeth forth much fruit." And they had been taught that this word is the law of life.

And so it was that Star and Supu began to be "plowed under."

24

The Mind of a Sunflower

WE were away together when Star received a long letter from her uncle who wanted to prevent an out-of-caste marriage. Supu had not been the chosen bridegroom, but he was preferable to anyone else. And now there was this foolish story afloat (for he had heard something of that talk in the jungle), and his Hindu-Christian mind protested. To begin with, the matter should not be settled by Star and Supu, but by their relatives. For the two concerned to have any opinion was unsuitable and absurd. Above all, it was perilous, for to what might it not lead? So he resolved to pull firmly at the cord of caste feeling doubtless fastened deep in the soul of this tiresome child, though she did not seem to realize it. He knew nothing of the mind of a sunflower ("They asked the Lover in what manner the heart of man was turned towards the love of his Beloved. He answered them and said: 'Even as the sunflower turns to the sun'"), so how could he understand the ways of "a mind freely borne into that which it sweetly loves"? With good hope, then, he pulled the cord. His letter began with the usual greeting, expressions of desire for news of his niece; and presently the hand was put forth and firmly gripped the cord.

"Whatever we let go in becoming Christians, it is, of course, understood that caste is not included in the list.

"To break caste by eating food cooked by one of a lower caste is objectionable, though sometimes necessary, for example, when one is being educated; for the sake of securing that education it may have to be done, but that is a thing which can be dropped when the object has been attained; it is a trifle as compared with breaking caste in marriage. That is the only thing that counts, for it is vital, it touches the root of the system; other caste breakings only crop off a leaf here and there." So the letter besought Star never to yield to any influence which would make her caste seem small to her, for God Himself had sanctioned the keeping of caste in marriage, by directing Abraham to take a wife from his own people. "I do not think my uncle knew that the people of Canaan were under a curse, which cannot be said of the Christians of other castes in Tinnevelly," is Star's comment. "But this was his view.

"I took the letter to my amma and read it to her, and she told me the story of Hezekiah, and then we spread the four sheets on the floor before the Lord, and asked Him to read them and to show me how to answer them. This was the first time I had heard of Hezekiah, and I was comforted as we did this. Then my amma told me to go and write whatever I believed God gave me to say to my uncle, and I went away alone, and this is the pith of the letter that I wrote:

"'I had thought you would have stood by me and would want me to live as a real Christian should, but you have written to me a letter which is weak in spirit. Please do not write to me at all if you cannot write strengthening letters.' This letter ended my trouble; my uncle understood it was vain to advise me on these lines. He continued to be friendly, but he ceased to try to direct my mind."

The letter that ended Star's trouble was more polite in Tamil than it sounds in English, for in Tamil one can so turn a sentence that it conveys the sense of such a matter without the offence. The uncle was not offended. He must have shivered with disapprobation, and he showed by a carefully arranged caste marriage on his own account what his opinions were. But he and his mother—the old lady of the Daniel story—agreed that Star was hopeless, and they left her in peace as beyond the pale. And yet the day came when that old lady turned to her granddaughter's Savior. She asked for Star's name to be given to her in baptism, and she died a believer in our Lord Jesus Christ.

And now we who loved the child watched her, wondering what the future held for her. By this time she had grown to understand the Christian view of life. She had read the story of Cana of Galilee. She had seen happy homes where husband and wife were one in service. Perhaps the day would come when these two could be united without anyone "throwing dust at the name of our holy God."

It was then (as we heard years afterwards) that Star's parents, wrought up to acute indignation, determined to insist on her return. They would wait for the heaven-sent opportunity of my furlough, for I would, of course, follow the excellent custom of white people and "go and come;" the time must be near.

So, with the patience of the country, they said nothing just then. Why disturb anyone's tranquillity? The child must be allowed to call herself a Christian. That was evident. But if once they had her in their own hands she would not be this kind of Christian, but the harmless kind.

And no more understanding the bonds that bound my heart and tied my feet than the parents understood the thoughts of God for their child, my dear home-people wrote expectantly. They are all in the land of everlasting brightness; they know now why I could not return. And I think that they understand.

25

And Nothing Hard

OF all the young Hindus who came out as Christians during those early years, only two men stood the finer tests. One of those was Supu. The other was Arul Dasan, Servant of Grace, the boy of the attic with the whitewashed pillars, now and for many years senior brother in our Fellowship. Temptations of the flesh and spirit are sown thickly in the way where such lads must walk. There is something like the suck of a whirlpool in every street and alley; and no clean public opinion can be counted on, anywhere, to help.

But just as many a sailor has found that the thought of the high purity of the stars seen on his watch at sea has come between him and the low evils of the ports, so the thought of this Star whom he loved came between Supu and every evil thing. And as he went on to know his God he learned to use his Shield.

We found that we had much to teach them both about various common things. For example, their attitude towards people of lowly birth was that of their clan. Star's father, Supu's uncle, had among his servants a poor peasant, who, when he swallowed a bone which stuck in his throat, was left to starve to death. Star's casual reference to the incident was unconcerned. She had thought nothing of it. No one had thought anything of it. Why should they? It was of no account. Our faithful servants and the village folk generally were treated by both boy and girl as though they were dust of the earth, an entirely negligible kind of dust. When Star came to understand what her Lord and Savior must feel about such an attitude of mind, and the behavior to which it led, she swung to the opposite extreme and upset the established order by larding the bewildered dhobies (the washermen of the family) with honorifics. If those great titles had been addressed to their donkeys they could not have been more taken aback.

The Christian feeling towards animals had also to be learned, for Hindu India's refusal to take life does not mean kindness to our poor friends or any sort of sympathy with them. Their fate is piteous everywhere.

There were many such readjustments required, for the way of the Lord Jesus is not learned in a day; but the sovereign virtue of truth was in both from the first. They were without wax—sincere. And in love there was no flaw.

I do not remember whether Supu was specially gifted or not. Probably not. As a general rule it is the women of his clan who are the more richly endowed. But the heavenly Musician can make music from a scale of very few notes. The old Gaelic scale had no fourth and no seventh.[3] *Auld Lang Syne* can be played in the black notes alone: God can make music with less than five notes.

Soon after that talk by the thorn bushes we trekked across from Great-Lake on the eastern side of the district to Dohnavur on the western, for a few months' work in the taluk of Four-Lakes; Star was with us, for her father had now recognized that a Greater than he had claimed her, and moved by a power that he could not understand he had yielded in so far that she was allowed to live with us. Supu and four other boys who had openly confessed Christ at home followed us, and on an evening, whose memory is colored still by the Alleluia sunset which glorified it, he and those four were baptized. Each boy chose a name with the word *Shining* in it: Shining of Life was Supu's new name. Star's father, who had narrowly observed all five, said that Supu was the one who would, in his opinion, go farthest. He was indeed to go far. But of how far he was to go we little thought as we returned home from the water, singing.

Within a week two of the five were dead. We were told they died of cholera (powdered glass or arsenic, who knows? said some under breath). Supu, the second to die, had gone to some relatives who lived in Red-Goddess, as that had seemed safe, and he was eager to share his gains. We had seen in him an evangelist to his own people and we had been full of hope for the clan. "Lord, help; maintain Thine own cause," wrote the Iyer in his journal the night that hope fell. We heard afterwards that as the Hindus stood round the boy when he lay dying, some mocking, some bewailing, he witnessed a good confession, and all undismayed he cried in a loud voice, out of the midst of tearing pain, quoting a line from a lyric: "Victory to Jesus' Name! Victory to Jesus!" and the people who heard him wondered.

"Christ truly does marvelously in His lovers, the which with a special and a perfect love He takes to Himself. Truly they desire not softness of the flesh or the beauty thereof; all worldly things they forget; they love not temporal prosperity nor dread the world's frowardness. Full sweet they think it to suffer for Christ, *and nothing hard*." Nor was it hard to Star; she had learned to trust the Love that had called her from her nest. But where your treasure is, there shall your heart be also; there was more of Star in heaven now that Supu was there.

26

Free to Follow the Call of the Spring

SOON after Supu's passing we took Star with us to Cape Comorin, and one day the Iyer proposed a sail in a katta-maram (a clumsy but unsinkable boat made of three logs tied together, hence its name—*katta*, to tie, *maram*, tree). We took the two girl converts for whose sake so many houses had been closed, Pearl, the senior sister of the women's band (she had only one arm), and our little Star. There was nothing to hold on to, and when we were half a mile from the shore a wave swept all five of us into the sea. I felt Star torn from beside me, found myself with one hand clinging to the log, the other flung out trying to reach her—she was just beyond me. In another moment a wave had washed her towards me, I had caught her hand, and the fishermen had pulled us in. Pearl and the two girls were in before I knew they had been out.

The fishermen who were sailing the katta-maram exclaimed in wonder. They said that we had escaped from three dangers. We might have been beaten under by the waves, or caught and crushed between our katta-maram and the second one (loosely lashed to ours), or snatched at by sharks. They proposed to turn back as the wind was rising. But we did not feel like that. The fishermen roped us in somehow, we sang a Tamil chorus—it was blown away by the wind—and we sailed gaily on; for when a thing that might happen does not happen, it is easy to forget how nearly it did happen.

But no one at home forgot, and when we returned to Dohnavur to find to our delight the boy, Arul Dasan, waiting there, at liberty at last to be a Christian, we found that the tale of our deliverance from drowning had preceded us. “It came to take the head and it took the turban only,” is what the Tamil says of a peril narrowly escaped. And that wave had not taken even a turban; we were quite unhurt. Even the one-armed Pearl had been protected. “The favorable influences of Venus attend them,” said the people, and Star’s father was deeply impressed. Surely the hand of the Supreme was in this matter. He had chosen his child to be His worshipper, and who could withstand Him? It was the hour for which we had waited; his heart was softened now. We asked and obtained his consent to her baptism. The bird must be allowed to follow the call of the Spring.

It was the evening of the eighth of March, 1901 (almost two years after that meeting by the well side), when we, who were back in Great-Lake again, walked together, singing and playing on tambourines and cymbals, through the palms to the shore of the water which gave the place its name.

From the temple nearby, two days before, a little girl had come to us, the first of a company of children undreamed of then. We had been so carefully directed in our journey from Dohnavur near the Western Ghauts, to our old headquarters on the plains of Vishnu’s-heaven, that we were there just in time to shelter little Pearl-eyes when she escaped from the clutches of the gods. She was the first child in Southern India, so far as is known, to escape like that. Thank God, she was not the last. I cannot look at this photograph of the door of the temple of Great-Lake without thinking of another door, “Behold a door opened in heaven,” and He whom the prisoner of Patmos saw when he looked through that door, He who sat on the throne, the Savior of the world, had said, “Let a door be opened on earth, a door out of the temples of India, and suffer the little children to come unto Me.” And it was so.

That child was with us then; she said nothing, but she watched everything with wonder.

This, only her second evening with Christians, was full of things not to be understood. Why did Star walk into the water and dip slowly under it just as though she was bathing? Only it was not at all like ordinary bathing, for the white man of the bungalow was with her—doing things, speaking words. Why? What did it all mean? This simple open-air ceremony was quite different from the secret hidden rites which she had seen performed in the dark depths of the temple. This was pure as the air. It was very beautiful, she thought.

It was indeed beautiful. The peaceful water was all soft silver, shifting lights and shadows, and faint blue-greys soon to kindle in a pale clear gold. We stood looking at it in stillness for a while before we sang again. "I am present, as a season of beauty upon the mountains." We had known Him so in Dohnavur under the mountains. "I am present, as a season of beauty upon the waters." We knew Him so in that lovely hour. And joy poured down upon us. Thy love is better than wine, Thy joy is better than wine. Far better than all the wine of earth, all beauties, powers, glories, is the joy that overflows like the overflowing of a fountain, from the joy in the presence of the angels of God.

Four months later, "because God had taken care of her in a cold place" (the Nilgiris, where we had gone for the hot weather), Star's father allowed her "to join the Holy Evening Meal," and so by his consent she became a full member of the household of God. And He who had fed her in the wilderness with manna which her fathers knew not, led her now into a good land, a land of brooks of water, of fountains and depths that spring out of valleys and hills.

27

Damascus Steel

BUT between those two quiet days, the days of her baptism and her first Communion, there was a day of turmoil. Again and again her father had come with his mind made up to take her home; for as Star, who was a child of few illusions, had foreseen, his resolve was not proof against the continual remonstrance of his womenfolk and the reproach of his clan. Now, three days after her baptism, Walker Iyer, under promise of safe conduct, took Star and the boy who had been tied to the pillar to see their people and witness to them. But the moment it was known that he and they were in the town hundreds of angry caste men filled the streets. They seized the bulls, pulled them out, thrashed the driver, and carried off the boy and girl, who were at once shut up where no one could have found them. "Keep the child now you have got her," urged Star's mother. And the women of that clan were not accustomed to have their word disputed, for they are of great importance; property is inherited on the women's side in Uncrowned-King, and girls are prized.

But Star's father was ashamed to break his pledged word to the Iyer; he would not allow his wife to "cause the child to disappear," though how the day would end he did not know.

Nor did the Englishman who stood in the heat and dust and noise, tired out, but never for one moment thinking of giving way. And he stayed himself upon his God.

At last the old headman, too frail to come out into the turbulent streets, called his son: "There is a white man in trouble. Go and help him in his need." (Long ago a white man had helped him in some trouble—illness, perhaps—and he had not forgotten.) But when his son plunged into that roaring mob he was dismayed. "The people are too strong for me! What can I do? I am but one." Then suddenly he took courage and shouted and flung himself into the fray. Some sided with him; the boy was hurriedly produced, then Star, and they were hustled into the bandy; the driver, all bruises and moans, was hoisted up on the driving board, the Iyer set himself firmly at the other end with his spoils of battle behind him, so that they could not be snatched out again without knocking him down first. And they all arrived home in safety.

So it was clear that such visits did not help. We had to wait till we could have Star's people in friendship, and they, in the loving and forgiving way of India, would welcome us as guests. That time had not come yet. And for several painful months she had to endure the cold misunderstanding and enmity of all her kindred, except of those who, one by one, began to follow her into the new life. Her father, who had once asked her to read with him and to pray for him, was tried beyond measure by these conversions, for they were, as all held, a stain on the fair fame of the clan. "Cursed be your feet that marked the way," he said in his anger and deep chagrin that a daughter of his could have so disgraced herself. The clan echoed that curse. It is terrible to be cursed.

But the swords that made their way from India through Damascus into Europe, and were then known as Damascus blades, were not wrought with ease or in a day. Just because it was appointed for high uses, that metal was plunged again and again into the furnace and beaten blow upon blow till at last the fine Damascus steel was forged, so strong and yet so flexible that (to quote Ivanhoe) Saladin could sever a gossamer veil thrown into the air by drawing his scimitar across it. There was no easier way then to forge and to temper that kind of steel, nor is there now, nor can ever be.

28

The Crimson Garment

I THINK my story must have made it plain that when man or woman, boy or girl dares to break through the opposing powers of death and hell and openly follow the Crucified, something inevitably and often immediately happens, as though to fling that life on the ground and stamp it underfoot. It is usually illness, or accident, something that looks like the hand of the avenging god. Then it is that the writing on the soul, invisible till now, appears, made legible, as it were, by the hot iron of this burning experience. One who understands that writing can read strange things there. "All night long the lizards cheeped" says much to one who knows the thought of the East.

But after the first assault has been repulsed there may be another, often many others, and so it was with Star. Twenty days after the day when for the first time she ate of the Bread and drank of the Wine, she was tossing in high fever, and the puzzled apothecary from the next village was suggesting a mixture of remedies, some Indian, some foreign; and we were beset behind and before by the clamors of relatives, who were sure beyond a doubt that this second illness was the signal sign of the wrath of the offended god.

It was typhoid fever; pneumonia followed; she all but died. First Supu, now Star. Was it strange that her family saw in such smashing blows an inescapable retribution, and trembled, asking, "What next?"

A friend came most lovingly then to help us nurse her, and we wrestled for her life. The word expresses that struggle. It was like fighting a tangible foe. It was never a wrestle with a reluctant Father (God forbid), but with His enemy and ours. I write this clearly because of the strange phrase, "wrestling with God," which is often used about such prayer. There is a wrestle, but it is with those all but palpable powers that seek to intervene between us and our God. And in the end we are given the desire of our hearts.

I know that sometimes we do not see how the thing granted is at all what we desire. And yet it is. (I write for lovers only.) For, after all, what the deepest in us wanted was not our own natural will, but the will of our Father. So what is given is our hearts' desire: He hath not withholden the request of our lips. *But God always answers us in the deeps, never in the shallows of our soul;* in hours of confusion, to remember this can help.

We had no doctor to pilot us through that illness, but a medically-minded missionary came several times and did all that he could for us. "Is it well with the child? It is well," he wrote across her chart when things were at their worst; and he said pitifully about me: "She will have to give her up." There were hours, day and night, when the only thing to be done was to hold on and refuse to let the frail little thread of her life slip through our fingers. There was one night—Star lay unconscious all that night—when in a shrine near the house the noise of tom-tom and cymbal sounded rampant in exultation over what seemed like another triumph for the gods. The weird shrieks of excited worshippers cut through the dark air between us and the shrine in a sort of fury, and there came a rush of voices that seemed to fill the room. But the peace of God was round about us. His peace was nearer than the noise, and so it continued to be all the time. When the child's parents came and stood by her cot waiting to break into the death wail, when their accusing eyes were upon us and we could explain nothing, words cannot tell what it was to be folded in the peace of God.

Star came back from the gates of death a fragile shadow of herself. Her long hair had been cut off, of course, and her curly head made her look like a boy. She was so light that I could pick her up in my arms, and often did, carrying her over the rough places when we went out in the evenings, and wishing in my heart that I could carry her so over all the rough roads of life—weak wish, and futile. Ours is a God who delivers, not from the hour of trial, but out of it, out of its power; and in the bearing up under it, not in the sliding out from beneath it, there is strength and victory. "'Say, O Lover,' asked the Beloved, 'if I double thy trials, wilt thou still be patient?' 'Yea,' answered the Lover, 'so that Thou double also my love.' The Beloved clothed Himself in the garments of His Lover, that he might be His companion in glory for ever. So the Lover desired to wear crimson garments daily, that his dress might be like that of his Beloved."

29

And Your Eyes Meet the Eyes of God

AFTER this illness Star's family became friendlier, and she greatly desired to go again to her old home. If only she could sit down among her people and show them once more what she had to offer, surely they would not refuse it. She was to go, and soon, for suddenly her father died. It was known that not long after he had cursed his child his mind had seemed to change; he had flung aside his accumulated merit, fruit of sacrificial gifts to the temple and of a life of careful observances of Hindu rites. All his honorable reputation, all his hopes, these had become as ashes to him; he worshipped the true God alone. But he had not yet openly confessed Christ. And now, as fatal illness seized him, his first thought was of Star. "She cannot come in time; do not write to her till I am gone" (for he knew that we were three hundred and fifty miles distant at the time), and he gathered the curtains of silence about his soul, utterly refusing priest, holy ashes, Hindu ritual, or any other sustaining hand through the dark valley. "No use, no use," he said. And then death came with awful swiftness, rushing upon him. But who knows the secrets of such an hour? There is One who can run more swiftly than Death. "When he was yet a great way off his father saw him and had compassion, and ran, and fell on his neck and kissed him; and the son said unto him, Father, I have sinned." Was that the story of the hour?

When he passed, the priest took possession—there was no one now to forbid—and the Brahmans feasted. By the time we got there (for we went as soon as we could) things had settled down into a tired-out quietness. Even the poor mother had hardly strength to rise to the customary wail; and the call of the little sisters to the spirit of their father, "Father, father, our sister has come," sounded weary.

It was a difficult day. Between those who know our Lord and those who do not there is a separation which no affection can cross. Star could not do all that was customary. She could not wail and beat her breast and tear her hair and knock her head upon the floor or against the wall, or thump it with her knuckles, so they thought her unfeeling. They did not know of tears at night as she woke up dreaming about her father. They thought she did not care, and this made her feel lonely.

There was loneliness outside, too, that curious, poignant loneliness which comes when you return to a place that once was home to you and now knows you no more. The very houses and streets were dear, but as she passed they had looked coldly upon her. She would have renewed her friendship with the old familiar things, but they said to her: "We do not belong to you now; you do not belong to us." Soon her sisters began to talk with half-mocking frivolity: "If thou wilt follow our caste customs, we will join the Way." And yet they were kind even to me. As they were ceremoniously unclean by the late presence of their dead in the house, they could touch both of us and caress us. The mother insisted on feeding me with her own hand, in the mother-to-child Indian way, pressing squeezed-up balls of curry and rice into my mouth, and she made me rest by her on her mat. But to Star it was always, "Nay, we do not wish to hear of thy Jesus Lord. Hast thou not written many letters to us? Is that not enough?" Little Mimosa, who would gladly have listened, was carefully prevented. The sisters chattered ceaselessly about matters of no moment. How could they do so? Star wondered. To her the house was full of thoughts of her father. How could they talk of these trivial things?

So she was solitary among them all. After a while, still hoping for an opportunity of showing her treasure, Star proposed a visit to a cousin who lived near. This cousin, like the girl in the Fort, being childless, was sitting in sadness. She had submitted to many austerities, but in vain. "Her husband deals in magic," someone told us, and story after story was half whispered, half gestured, never with any sense of surprise or untruth, but always under breath, as though in fear that someone unseen might overhear, for India is a cabinet of drawers, and secret drawers. "See," said one, pointing fearfully to a heap of rags in a corner of the room where we sat, "it is there—the *kurali* is there."

This particular charm is made of the bones of a firstborn child. It is a thing of cold horror to the people; I have never heard it lightly mentioned. To the casual eye it is a mere doll, hideous, dirty, insignificant; but there is something loathly and Satanic about it. And this is not imagination; it is a true insight which sees in that trifle something that is not trivial. The rulers of this darkness are not phantoms of the mist.

Does this sound archaic? Among us today is a young Brahman woman in whose eyes still lingers the tragic look that tells of a soul brought face to face with the underworld. A few days ago, a converted sorcerer gave his magical properties to one of the brothers of this Fellowship, asking him (he dared not do it himself) to destroy them; so they were burned in the House of Prayer. Among them was the *kurali*. The house was full of children breathlessly watching the flame leap almost to the roof. To them it was only flame; but to the young mother who sat among them it was far more. "I seemed to see my little daughter's face ascending in that flame," she said, and she told us of how among her husband's friends was a celebrated sorcerer. He often came to the house and petted her baby daughter—her little firstborn. The child was ten months old and full of charming ways, and he would fondle her in a possessive fashion which alarmed her mother. Three times he all but carried her off on some pretext or other to his own house; but each time the mother contrived to circumvent him. She was thankful when her husband decided to live in another town. She felt safer there. Soon after the family had moved she heard that the sorcerer had made friends with another baby girl, who had suddenly died. And though she could not have proved it, she felt sure that her little one was a bird escaped from the snare of the fowler.

This page helps to make the background for a story which sets its roots in fact. Everywhere now, as everywhere years ago, we find courteous attention when we gather the educated to listen to the Gospel. But deep down, far out of sight of the speaker, is the ancient life of this ancient land. And the heart breaks into the old, old cry, Oh that Thou wouldest rend the heavens, that Thou wouldest come down, that the mountains might flow down at Thy presence! Most righteous God, O God of Love, so let it be.

We did not get very far that day, for good listening alone does not content those whose expectations reach beyond that, and for Star the unsatisfied longing over her people clouded her sky as we said our farewells. But our Father is never nearer than in a cloudy evening, and we looked at the bow set in the cloud, *"And the bow shall be in the cloud: and I will look upon it.* And God looks at the bow, and you look at the bow, and your eyes meet the eyes of God."

30

Under the Tamarind Tree in the Fort

WE stopped at the Fort on our way home. Again there was the unchanging silence. The very sunshine seemed stiller here than outside. We found our way to the shadiest street, and waited awhile, but no one came. So we went on, found a deserted house in good repair, explored its rooms through barred windows; went on, saw signs of people, but saw no one; only a black goat wandered about, the sparrows chirped and squirrels darted across the path.

We ventured to knock at last. A woman's voice called out to us, "There is death in the house!" It was not the time for a visit.

We found an awning of mats where four ways met, and waited, wondering if anyone would come.

By this time we had learned more of the life of the people. The old law which allowed only one daughter to a family (any others must be killed) had drained the clan of women, and now their great desire was to persuade fellow caste men outside to let their daughters intermarry with sons of the Fort. They were rich enough to offer large sums of money for suitable maidens (they had built a rest house for travellers on the riverbank, and all knew of their prosperity), but no one could be persuaded to send a daughter into lifelong captivity. Her mother and sisters might see her again, her father and brothers never. As for the girls themselves, the thought of being given to the Fort was a nightmare. So thus far all negotiations had failed, and rather than yield and let their women live a normal life, the clan was content to perish slowly; so firmly do these people hug their chains. For they are not as others are. Long ago their ancestors used to crown the sovereign of the South Country. (In memory of this their men crown the god in the chief temple at Tinnevelly at one of the annual festivals.) Some years ago a friendly Governor of the Province with his suite drew up outside the door through which we had walked, and asked to be allowed to go in. But he was turned back, and neither he nor any man has ever broken the law of that handful of resolute people. A small allowance is paid yearly by Government towards the upkeep of "this odd Fort"; to most it is just that. But a hundred men, women, and children, without hope and without God in the world, are something more than merely odd. We thought of that as we waited there.

Presently some of the little girls of the place, dainty fascinating children, came to us shyly, and we made friends with them. A servant passed, flattening himself against the wall before he got within contaminating radius. The children drew their small garments close about them lest his shadow should fall on them and defile them. The man shrivelled up in his servility. And yet he too was a caste man, for no other could be servant to these aristocrats. The children glanced at him not unkindly, but the arrogance of centuries was stamped upon their little faces then.

After a while they left us, and we went to one of the tamarind trees near the door, and kneeling there prayed for the place as we had never prayed before.

31

The Cross with the Sword in its Heart

THE Southern Cross, last seen in the horizon of Jerusalem at the time our Lord was crucified,[4] shines in our South Indian sky early on the morning of Christmas Day. At other seasons we can see it slowly rising till it hangs quite straight, and then setting behind the mountains. Following the Cross is the Scorpion trailing his long length halfway across the sky; he seems to be trying to overtake the Cross, but he never does. It reminds the watcher of that vision in the book of Revelation, of the great red dragon who waited to devour the newborn child; but the child was caught up to God and to His throne. There are times when these two mighty pageants show the truth about this war of the ages more clearly than words ever could. Even a young girl is an object of malevolence to the powers that are against us. And the Cross as we know it is a Cross with a sword set in its heart. "As the Father hath loved me, I also love you, said I to my disciple, whom certainly I did not send to temporal joys, but to great conflicts; not to honors, but to contempt; not to ease, but to toils; not to rest, but to bring forth much fruit in patience. Remember these words, my son"—a Cross with a sword in its heart.

A few months after the death of Star's father, her mother, brother, aunts, uncles, and cousins came in force to Dohnavur, which was now home to us. With great determination these relatives set themselves to persuade or coerce her to agree to a marriage with a youth called Effulgence, for whom she had not and never would have the slightest affection.

There was no way to make things easier for her. To prepare a pleasant meal for them would have been to entangle a courteous people in discourtesy, for they could not have accepted it. They might not even drink water from our well. Caste interfered there, as it does so often, withering by its very presence those little gentle kindnesses that do so much to sweeten difficult occasions. Tired after their journey, and entirely implacable, they sat in a circle round Star, who was, of course, alone among them when they brought all their batteries to bear upon her; for it was important that we should not appear to influence or to interfere.

But we were in communication, though out of sight and out of sound: "What is the secret of communication between animals? Giraffes are known to be utterly silent; no one has ever heard them utter the slightest sound. Yet if one giraffe is separated by a hill from the sight of the herd to which he belongs, and that herd takes alarm, the single giraffe knows instantly, and gallops to join the others. I do not think we can account for this by suggesting the existence of a sound vibration, to which our ears are not attuned; we seem compelled to fall back upon some wave of thought which is used by certain of the animals, although unknown to ourselves."[5]

But is it quite unknown to ourselves?

We cannot explain many things which we know to be facts; we have "little knowledge and only a great deal of wonderment" where they are concerned. But there is a strange power born of love, nourished on love, by which we may know as much as we need to know, in order that we may help by prayer. As though alongside that assaulted child—she was only sixteen—we understood her need through those tempestuous hours.

Among the pastors of the district was an excellent man who had a concern to deal with Star about this matter, so presently she had a letter:

"I have heard of thy refusal to wed Effulgence, that earnest devout convert—a servant of God.

"Hast thou ever heard of an Indian girl who lived an unmarried life?" (India, even South India, is a large word. There may have been such, but no one here knew them.) "Should thy amma die tomorrow, who would take care of thee? Perhaps thou wilt say, 'God will take care of me. I want to give myself to the children, and to save others for His kingdom'— but what about this man? If thou dost not marry him he will return to Hinduism; then his blood will be on thy head. We cannot enter into the Kingdom with bloody hands." (This is slightly mixed, but as he wrote it.) "What does the Bible say? 'For how knowest thou, O wife, whether thou shalt save thy husband?'

"Perhaps thou art thinking that if thou art married, thou canst not give all thou hast to the children." (Star was at that time preparing to do this.) "Think of Moses. What that one man did no woman could have done." (The pastor evidently took it for granted that we should absorb Effulgence and use him in the work, for he did not understand about building in gold, silver, precious stones, or that Effulgence could not help us in that kind of building.) "When God created Adam He gave him Eve. Who sinned? It was not the man. A woman is a weak thing. Thou art still young. It is very difficult for thee to realize thine own weakness. And consider him, Effulgence; thou knowest him, his preaching, how wonderfully he prays, and what a beautiful, handsome lad he is. I need not describe his personality, thou knowest it all."

Star wrote, as was meet, thanks for the pastor's care and interest: "But when I read your letter these words came to me. 'Be not fastened together in a strange yoke with the faithless'" (for she could not share the general view of Effulgence). "Will you please read Second Corinthians 6:14, to the end? Graciously forgive me who am so young for asking you to do so. The verse you quoted, I do not take for myself, for he is not my husband, so I am not his wife." The Moses argument left her unshaken: "God does not need Uzziah's hand to take care of the Ark. 'I saw the Son of Man sitting on the throne of God.' The Son of Man came to seek and save the lost lambs. I have the Man, Christ Jesus." Her letter written, she fled from the talk of the world to her Lord who understood:

Rose of my heart, what seek I now but Thee?
And dost Thou say, Thorns grow upon My Tree?

Thorns tore Thee, Fairest, what if I be torn?
Where Thou dost blossom who would stay for thorn?

I hold Thee fast: I will not let Thee go,
For me doth this dear Rose of roses blow.

And so I say, Rose of my heart, to Thee,
Close by my Rose would I Thy lover be.

• • •

We had just settled down peacefully after these various agitations when a retired Indian lawyer, a Christian, much respected and accustomed to deference, came to stay with us at Dohnavur. "I wish to interview the young girl alone," he said. So alone she went to Walker Iyer's little study and stood before him. He told her how glad he had been to hear of her conversion, but how astonished to hear of her contumacy. He knew Effulgence, a nice boy, most suitable. "Thou art doing wrong. Dost thou think that thou canst live like thy amma? Thou canst not. White people are quite different from us. Theirs is a Christian country, and very small. Very few men are there. If thou wert in England today thou wouldst see many unmarried women; perhaps one in ten lives so. They are not living that life for Christ's sake. It is their custom. But in India no woman can live without marrying. It is not their custom. Hast thou ever heard of any?"

"I have not heard of any, but—" and Star began to try to explain. She was soon interrupted:

"Thou thinkest only of thyself. What about thy people? If thou dost marry Effulgence how happy they will be! A day will come when thou wilt think, 'Would that I had married him!' but by that time he will be back in Hinduism. If thy thought be to follow Christ, remember what He said to the demoniac who wanted to follow Him. 'Jesus suffered him not, but saith to him, Go home to thy friends and tell them how great things the Lord hath done for thee.'" (Star had, as we know, gone home to her friends, and she hoped to do so again, but that was not the point. "Conform to their wishes, otherwise they will not receive thee," *that* was what she was meant to understand.) "Do not think lightly of my words," continued the courtly old gentleman. "Do not think my advice is like that of other men. *My words cost money*. If I were to speak professionally I should be paid for all these words." And with a dignified wave of the hand he closed the interview.

Then to Star came what she calls the slash of a poisoned knife. What did that verse which the lawyer had quoted mean? Suddenly his final argument restored her to peace: My words cost money, he had said, "but the word that my Lord Jesus spoke to me cost Him His life. At once I found my feet on the Rock."

The end of Effulgence was tragic. He went to Ceylon, got work in a mission there and married into a good family but out of caste, as many do in that more enlightened island. His people objected. Fearing their displeasure, he wrote denying his marriage and promising to return to India and marry in caste. Thereupon his young wife died. There were suspicions of foul dealing, but no proof. Effulgence returned to his own town, and in order to disgrace Star's family because of her refusal, he caught her little sister, a child of eight or nine, as she was returning from the well, carried her off to a house nearby, and tied a tali (marriage symbol) round her neck. The child cried out, and the people round about heard and ran to rescue her. Effulgence fled. Then the child snatched the tali off, swung it round her head three times, and flung it on the ground. Effulgence, still bent on publicly disgracing the family, accused Star's mother of refusing to restore his bride; and he filed a suit against her.

Meanwhile Star had a snowstorm of letters. This was her doing. Let her look at the fruit of her obstinacy and repent. She felt it all keenly: her father was not there to help her mother now, and she had this trouble for her sake. Very earnestly she asked her heavenly Father to stand by her poor mother.

But she was pricked as by sharp spears. "Is this Christ's love or virtue to thy widowed mother?" was the question of all. She was ready to go through anything for His name's sake, but could she bear it if her little sister were to be disgraced for her whole life? And she prayed to the God of battles to fight for her little sister. One night she could not sleep. Torturing pictures of the child's future, perhaps to be a stained future, passed before her. Next day a letter came to her from her mother. It was the first time she had ever written to Star: "My child, Effulgence is threatening to go to the High Court. I am writing this to tell thee not to be troubled about thy sister's future. Not for one moment was she alone in his hand. All the children of the street were there, as well as older people. She will be happily married when the right time comes. Effulgence has wealth to fight in the Courts, but thou hast the Lord thy God. Pray to thy God that we may win. He knows that we are innocent."

To have experience of Indian Courts is to be brought close to Lowell's, Careless seems the Great Avenger,

> Truth for ever on the scaffold, Wrong for ever on the throne,
> Yet that scaffold sways the future, and, behind the dim
> unknown,
> Standeth God within the shadow, keeping watch above His own.

That He is within the shadow is the very anchor of the soul, but it is a blessed thing to see Truth come down from the scaffold. That blessing was granted then, and for that day at least, Truth was enthroned in Uncrowned-King, for Effulgence lost his suit, worshipped Siva, and married a Hindu. His relapse brought another snowstorm: "Now his blood is on thy head. Thou wilt have to account to God for his soul."

It was thus (later when the same question came in more attractive form it was answered in the same way, because Star had heard another Voice) that the path was opened through the jungle of prejudice, custom, and the ignorance born of fallacious interpretation of Scripture. That track has been followed by many. But few know what it cost to blaze the trail.

Still it has been blazed; and now, even in this conservative corner of South India, it has come to be understood that such a path is possible, and that our Lord does sometimes choose that His child shall walk in it. Why was it ever forgotten, I wonder? All down the ages, from castle and cottage, He whom our soul loveth has called some of His lovers to follow in this way. And to the one who heard the call and followed, He has spoken a secret word and shown a secret sign. And the happy lover has answered, *"Rose of my heart, what seek I now but Thee?"*

Perhaps because there are so many perishing for lack of love in a world which can be hard and cold to birds which have no nest of their own, He wants some mother-hearts to be free to make nests for them, just as He wants some of His knights to be St. Pauls, and some Sir Galahads. And for Francis of Assisi there is need everywhere.

32

Clay to Crystal

IN our mountain ravine stones are found unlike the stones in the near valleys. One of our Fellowship, whose special subject is geology, tells us what they are. A fragment of metamorphic rock, broken in half, shows mica and quartz in frosted crystals, and molybdenite in silver crystals, iron pyrites like gold, and little pink garnets in bright clusters. Another lovely stone is full of azurite, the blue veins running through a field of snow. The stone outside looks quite ordinary, mere water-worn brown, though, if you hold it to the light, you may see sudden sparkles, as of dust of silver or gold or copper. But for that sparkle there is nothing to tell of the fire that has made what was once a lump of clay into a treasure-mine of jewels.

Can I show the work of our God (who is the very Fire of Love) in the heart and character of this child, so that what is shown will waken wonder, not at the crystal and the color in the stone, but at that which wrought the beauty from mere clay?

The time when, in a special and definite manner, Star was taught not to shrink from that fire, but to open her whole being to its power, was the day when she was called to help in the common work of an ordinary nursery, and, like Brother Lawrence in his kitchen, do little things for the love of God. I mark this occasion because of the feeling which seems to be almost universal, in spite of that brother's witness to the contrary, that God's best is reserved for those who live apart from common things; and as most of us must attend to them it seems a pity that this thought should be so usual.

Rolle sets it forth with disarming plainness. Speaking of the Song of Songs, and the chariot mentioned there, he says the active are like the silver pillars; in conversation they are clear and in preaching full of sound; but the contemplative are like the golden seat; they offer rest to Him, and in Him singularly rest. "For to fulfil bodily service and nevertheless feel the heavenly sound and be melted in singing into the joy of heavenly love—I wot not if ever any mortal man had this. To me it seems impossible that both should be." But why?

Star at least was not troubled by that question, for she had not been brought up on the thought of the Middle Ages, or of the twentieth century either, but (as nearly as we know it) on His who walked the dusty roads of Palestine; and so, when the call came to that common work, it never crossed her mind that it would make any difference to the inner life of love, to which she had given herself from the first hour when the Light of Life burst upon her. She had now had four years of steady teaching. She was an eager reader, had found her way into many odd pockets of knowledge, and to her delight she had been allowed to attend the Iyer's Divinity classes; for, young as she was, she was able to follow those enriching Tamil Bible studies on which he nurtured his students. Star, on her mat at the door of the little verandah room of the Dohnavur bungalow, half hidden by the big blackboard, learned as much, perhaps, as the men. She was, at any rate, as keen. For the last few months she had been given another joy. Chaperoned by an older woman she went out to the villages in the afternoons. It was a happy life; those walks were all Emmaus walks, for the elder woman, like the younger, was a loving disciple, and to such Jesus Himself draws near, and their hearts burn within them while He talks with them by the way. One afternoon they visited a house full of smallpox, but that disease is more or less ever with us, and no one happened to mention it.

Just then in our Nursery in Neyyoor in Travancore, there was a sudden and urgent need of help. We had no one to give but Star, so I took her. The call had come unexpectedly, and she had only a few minutes to pack her things before we were off; but in the long, slow journey she had time to think, and then came a strong temptation; it swept up like a wave.

Will those who have not been stripped and scourged as Star had been understand her? The possibility had never been absent from our minds that her people might yield to the pressure of the clan, and claim her, and my chief thought had been to fortify her for whatever life might bring. So she had been constantly with me, and we had grown together as palm trees in this country often do when their roots have become inextricably united; as body and spirit, as flower and scent, to quote from the Tamil, so indeed we were united.

It was not the first sweep of that wave. When she first came to live with us Star shared my room; later she had a side room opening off it. But the time came when the side room was needed for bungalow uses, and so I had prepared another room for her, not so near, but the nearest possible. Among old records which somehow have escaped destruction is a little blue diary, much older than the notebook from which I have quoted in earlier chapters. Star had begun to learn English about that time, and her entries in it are in our baffling tongue. They are too private for much quotation, but a few of the less intimate will show with the simplicity of utter truth how the smallest frets of common life may be used to discover the clay.

For her new room had seemed far away, and her "qruwal flesh," as she called it, had rebelled. "I never had it like this before, to leave my mother, but Thou art my mother bird;" for the poor heart did valiantly try to comfort itself, though the "qruwal flesh caught like a hook," and there was no real joy or victory yet. "Lord, it is a little easier," is the relieved entry a few days later, "but O my Father, soon unhook it from me"; and again, "O Spirit of the Lord, lift up a standard against my qruwal flesh." I had filled the new room with little things I knew that she would like to have, just to welcome her, but these had seemed to add to the burden. She would look up gratefully from something I had hoped would be a happy surprise, and her eyes would slowly fill with tears, till, distressed and wholly unable to imagine why it should be so, I could only try to love her out of her trouble, whatever it was. At last she told me about it. The dearer the little gifts, the more distant and more final the banishment had felt, for with the finding of each new tiny treasure there had been a whisper, *"Abraham gave them gifts and sent them away."*

We had laughed very tenderly together over that, and I was sure that my dear child would recognize the deceiver next time he came dressed as an angel of light, even though he whispered texts. But the stern lesson of life—that we are not here to enjoy one another—had this been quite mastered? I was not sure. I should not have chosen just that time for that lesson. The Effulgence episode had been a strain: I had hoped for smooth going for a while; but the love of God is courageous. And so, as the bandy trundled slowly along the road under the hills, I opened this matter to her.

"But He gave you to me for my own-of-owns," said Star in that weak moment, and never had the Tamil word sounded so full of yearning. Its five small syllables were like the five small fingers of a child clinging, refusing to let go. Must her soul be even as the weaned child and learn to do without?

Am I not enough, Mine own?
  Enough, Mine own, for thee?
Am I not enough, Mine own?
  I, for ever and alone,
I, needing thee?

That was the word for us then. And we talked of the difference between the fleshly love and the spiritual; the two loves stood out in sharp distinction. In such an hour the fire of the love of

God is searching. It knows just where to find the clay in us. That clay must be turned to crystal. Would we have it otherwise?

Next morning, as the bulls' heads were turned homeward, Star, standing in the street by the gate of the house which we had rented for a nursery, sent me off with a smile. It was a victory complete and final. Never again was the question raised; the Lord and His work came first, would always come first. The little book of the Lover and the Beloved puts it in a sentence of wrought gold: *"The will of the Lover left him and flew to the Beloved, and the Beloved gave it into the captivity of the Lover, that he might use it to love and serve Him."*

I never had a happier letter than the first letter Star wrote to me after the day when her will flew to the Beloved, for "Love clothed the heart of the Lover with thoughts of delight." To love Him far beyond all created things is never to be desolate. "Among all that are dear to thee, let Jhesu be solely thy darling and thy special friend" if thou wouldst have Him feed thee with the finest of the wheat, and satisfy thee with honey out of the rock.

Love songs were born from that experience, and others of a like nature. For it is possible to fulfil bodily service and nevertheless to "feel the heavenly sound and be melted in singing into the joy of heavenly love." In the Tamil this little song turns on a single verb, connoting union, harmony, communion, fellowship. The pleasance, lotus, and shadowy garden are India's words for loveliness and peace. But translations are withered leaves:

O Jesus Lord, Lord of my house of life,
Thou hast come near and oned me with Thyself.

O Jesus Lord, in common work, in pain,
To harmonize (my spirit) Thou hast come.

O Jesus Lord, in all times Thou hast come,
That I be knit in Thy communion.

O Lord, my Pleasance, Lord, my Lotus-flower,
Me hast Thou drawn into Thy fellowship.

O Shadowy Garden, my Redeemer pure,
Thee, Thee, I worship, Thee do I adore.

Never, never need we fear that common work will come between the Master and the servant (written so, how foolish it appears; are we far in spirit from a dear child who delights to do our will?). Only, there must be the welcoming of the fire that turns the clay in us to crystal.

Years have passed since Star stood by the gate of the little house which was our Nursery, and sent me off with a smile; but we both look back to that day as to a day set apart, memorable, whose sweetness can never be described.

And that day, I think, taught Star gentleness towards human weakness. There were deep wells of love in her, but her character was formed on strong lines, and she had never found it easy to understand weakness of any kind. "Ten Commandments" was our name for her as a child; she leaned towards law. And so all this was part of her preparation that she might be able in her measure to follow her Lord who suffered being tempted, and is able to succor them that are tempted. "For the power of sympathy lies not in the mere capacity for feeling, but in the lessons of experience. . . . He who yields to temptation has not known its uttermost force." Star had to know what it was almost to fall, and yet to be kept from falling. "Temptation openeth what we be," and temptation vanquished by the grace of the Lord does wonderfully gentle the heart and teach it compassion, till it is lowly enough to enter into the wise old words, "Be not hard to him that is tempted, but give him comfort, as thou wouldst will to be done to thee," considering thyself lest thou also be tempted.

33

Figures of the True

WHILE this story was being shaped two packets of photographs came from Munich and from Innsbruck. I had been wondering how I could tell in a few words something of what we had learned by watching our Lord's way with His little lover, for the help of others to whom also is committed the delicate charge of souls. Among the photographs were some which said what I wanted to say more clearly and more perfectly than I could. For to us all occur the same temptations. We have been given a young, dear life to tend. And as the soft willow catkins are set round the fragile upright beauty of this lily of the valley, so would the softness of our protective love gather round the precious thing that is a newborn soul. And God says, "No, I want that soul to prove its power to live an unprotected life. I want it to be a thing of wonder like this little wintergreen in its pocket of poor soil among the rocks."

"I often plant My flowers," He says, "among rough rocks."

And we acquiesce. We say, "Yes, Lord; I will not interfere. Thou shalt plant Thy flower where Thou wilt, and nourish it as Thou wilt. I will fear no evil, for Thou art with Thy flower." And then again, or ever we are aware, we have carefully set our treasure in some safe, sheltered place, even as these Christmas roses are set in a glass of water out of reach of sharp winds and cold snows. And again God says, "No, I want My souls to be like My wild strawberries and My ferns that live triumphantly out in the open, with the common air about them, and the common grass at their feet. Let Me have My way with them, and thou shalt see what I will do."

There are times when words are like clumsy fingers. Perhaps that is why so many types and shadows are fashioned for us. The world is full of them. Aaron's rod that budded is not the only stem that has budded for the reinforcement of faith. And he who sees takes off his shoes.

• • •

The next letter from Neyyoor was not from Star. It was from Ponnamal (Golden), the heroic Indian sister who was in charge of the children there. It told us that Star had smallpox and had been taken from the Nursery and put in an isolation hut.

My first thought was to fly to her (flight is not the word for crawling by bullock cart; it only expresses desires, and, counted by hours of travel, Neyyoor was further from us than Marseilles is from London). My second thought ran like this: The love of God is brave. My love would never have allowed this to happen, just after she had won that victory too, on her private battlefield. It is splendid to know that one's child is trusted like that. This view of the matter reversed my natural feelings and "mirthed my mind" so that I could be happy not to go to Star. For I could not go. There were many young children to care for and no one to leave in charge. The help that has been given now was far out of sight then. There were threatenings of trouble too; there always were in those days of beginnings, and they could not be left to swell to a formidable thunder. There was no possible way to go to my little Star.

Meanwhile the doctors, hoping to protect the babies in the crowded house in Neyyoor, had put up a palm-leaf shelter for Star outside the hospital grounds and appointed a woman to nurse her.

Now we in India do not take infection seriously. We know that doctors do—it is one of their many strange whims—and we humour them, for if we do not they are apt to be ruffled, and we do not like to ruffle such kind and generally useful people. So we are content to appear to obey their futile commands, though we cannot help knowing, of course, that the matter over which they agitate themselves is in other hands than theirs. We call those hands vaguely by various names according to our creed, though if we are Hindu, or Hindu-Christian, what we really mean is *vithi* (fate), that which is scored on the bone of our foreheads, as anyone can see who examines a skull on the burning ground. Our *vithi* is as inseparable from us as our shadow; a score of proverbs say so, and proverbs are always true.

So the woman appointed by the doctors, who was also, unknown to them, cooking for the students attending the hospital, continued to cook as usual, and as usual, friendly soul that she was, to mingle cheerily in the life of the place. And the doctors, as usual also, were far too busy to see what their cook women were about. So nobody's feelings were hurt.

But this meant that Star was alone for several hours every day, and there was one who knew it. This snake in the grass had a slimy habit of gliding round that but when the cook woman was immersed in her labors elsewhere, and being, as was supposed, very religious, he would approach the door with an unctuous "Little sister! May I come and sing a hymn with thee?" There were only palms round that hut. There were no houses within sight. There was no help within call. But Star was not alone; the Lord God who once prepared gourd, worm, and vehement east wind to serve His purpose, now prepared a dog, a poor despised pariah dog, to be her faithful guard, and all day long he lay on her cot at her feet; he never left her. When the voice, soft as butter, was heard outside, there would be a low growl from that dog; if the voice persisted, a sharp bark. The snake did not wait for more. Day after day he came gliding round the hut, but he never dared to come in.

When later I heard this, I was glad for once that it is not possible to see what is going on where our dearest are concerned, for how could I have done my work in Dohnavur—and it had to be done—had I seen that snake creeping up to the hut? But perhaps if we could see such things we should be allowed to see something else, even the angel guard, and I am very sure that if I had I should have asked one of them to pat that dog for me.

• • •

By this time it had become plain that Star was called to a service which would ask for all that she had to give. In Southern India, temple and dramatic societies (evil, and leading to evil) held out their hands for young children, as they have for uncounted generations, and as they do today. We had been appointed to save such children—girls and boys. Star was to be sister to companies of both, and so, perhaps that she might be more tenderly "touched with the feeling" of their need, there came another day when, very far away from the help of man (as these young children are) and unprotected by even a faithful dog, she was to taste the cup of fear and be (just as they are) the target of the destroyer.

She was in Ceylon and was staying with friends when that cup was forced into her hands. No one there knew of the danger; it was as unexpected as it was deadly, and the circumstances were such that a word spoken there, or even a word written to us in India, might have wrecked the happiness of several innocent people. So Star spoke no word in Ceylon, nor did she write to us. But when she returned in safety (for the Lord her God was her Present Help; He compassed her as with a shield), and in the privacy of home told of her experience, the Iyer, who recognized in one startled moment how near to her that peril had been, turned white. We could hardly hasten quickly enough to the end with its blessed "All's well." Who is offended and I burn not?

"In order to produce a movement of a vital, spiritual nature *someone must suffer*," said Josephine Butler in one of her many moments of vision. "Someone must go through sore travail of soul before a living movement, outwardly visible, can be born." The living movement for the salvation of threatened children had already been born, but there was still to be sore travail of soul for those who were ordained to give their lives to nothing less than the spiritual salvation of these children. This, more than any hour that had been before, was the hour of Star's travail, the hour, perhaps, of her ordination: "Mine the mighty ordination of the Pierced Hands." It was the hour when she came to understand in a new sense something of what it must have been to the Holy One to come in direct contact with sin, stark sin. Calvary had meant *that*.

Silver birch alone in the wind, little flower and fern nourished wherever they be planted, corn of the joy of the harvest from plowed land—each one severally "showeth His handiwork." Our pictures are figures of the true.

34

A Vein of Gold

BUT my thought is not to tell the life story of one who is still with us, fellow lover, fellow worker, but only to tell her child story for the comfort and joy of lovers of children and for those whose absorbing occupation is the nurture of a spiritual family, the spiritual training of souls. I have crossed my intended limits. My story has been caught like a small boat in the current of the lough that sets towards the bar; and the boat has all but crossed the bar. It is tempting to sail for a while in the open sea. I should like to tell of what has happened during these later years here in our family of Dohnavur and in Uncrowned-King, where Star's mother found peace in believing and her little sister Mimosa walked the Enoch walk. But a word must suffice: "Thou preventest him [surprisest him] with the blessings of goodness." That shows it. Can the cloud of witnesses be surprised? Hardly, I suppose, for the heavenly people have seen so many of the Father's loving deeds that nothing He can do can surprise them; but they must look on with a very lovely pleasure as He surprises with blessings of goodness His Stars and His Mimosas. For this dear Mimosa there came a day when she stood rapt in speechless joy and watched her husband receive his new name—Mercy of God. Had our eyes been opened as he came up out of the water, should we have seen his patient angel rejoicing with her and with us, above all with his Lord? I think so; for it cannot be that the angels of our childhood forsake us when we grow up. And others from Star's clan have followed her into the kingdom of light, never in crowds—that is not the way of the men and women of this story—but one by one. "Conform to the custom of the world, lest thou be hindered in thy service;" many had said that to Star. But she had heard another word: "Stand thou at My well-pleasing and thou shalt suffer no hindering." Our God asks for faithfulness, not for compromise: *Sow not thy field with mingled seed.*

But to count the blades of the springing corn or even the yellowing ears that seem so near to ripening is often perilous. It is better to wait till there is no need any more to fear the heat of the sun for the young green shoots, or the floods that can beat down the grain that was all but harvested. There are men and women now in India who walk about with Siva's ashes on their forehead or Vishnu's footmark painted there because—as it seems to us—too great a publicity in their early days of discipleship was caused to blaze upon them.

And now I hasten on with a hope that perhaps I may be allowed to bring comfort to one who has been disappointed and so is discouraged in prayer because something asked has not been given yet.

I have told of how a sense of the familiar in the people of the Fort had often been with me. One day I read a story in a Tamil manuscript. It told of two wealthy sisters, who with their retainers travelled south, more than eight hundred years ago, till they came to the Copper-Colored River. This river runs deep and swift after the Rains, but was fordable then. The sisters stood on the sandy bank and argued about how it should be crossed. One sister said: "Let the sari be lifted a little for the sake of convenience." The other said: "Not so; that would be indecorous and not according to custom. Let the sari cling about the feet." So one sister marched through the water holding her sari up, and the other drifted slowly through, letting her sari trail. The straw became a pillar, as the Tamils say, and the sisters parted in bitterness. They never met again. The sister who trailed her sari set her retainers to build a mud wall a mile long, fifteen feet high, and six feet broad, round some ground not far from the river. The wall was pierced with four doors, iron-bossed and fitted with huge locks. Within this wall it was then ordained the women-folk must dwell in absolute seclusion. No woman (except a servant) born within should ever go out alive. No man (except a servant) born without should ever come in.

The sister who had pluck and grit enough to break through a foolish custom went further and founded a town. Her people scattered through the Vishnu's-heaven taluk and became a vigorous and prosperous community. "And it is affirmed that the characteristic shown by the sister at the ford, who dared to act as she chose, apart from the rules of etiquette, still lingers in the family, for the women are brave and independent of spirit, and their men are very bold." So reads the Tamil manuscript (from which the story comes) and ends.

For a moment I saw nothing and put the paper down; then suddenly I understood, caught the clue that had eluded me so long, knew why that Fort woman's face had followed me and haunted me; for the town the courageous sister had founded was Uncrowned-King. It was their common ancestor who had crowned the King of the South Country in very olden days. Town and fort belonged to the same clan.

• • •

But to read of a vein of gold where no gold was known to be is not the same as to see it suddenly shine as the pick strikes common rock and lays bare the nugget or the bright gold thread. And yet I hope that my vein of gold may have something for others.

For in that moment of discovery I saw the two communities, not as two separate entities, but as they really were, one clan. So prayer for the one was prayer for the other. This meant that when nothing seemed to be happening in the Fort, something was being done for its help, for blessing in one part of the clan would surely lead to blessing in the other. Our prayer had not lost its way in the void.

So the old Tamil story discovered to me a golden thread of thought. The God who worketh for him that waiteth for Him is continually preparing the way for a larger answer to our prayer than we had imagined, and influences are being fashioned (and who can confine a spiritual influence?) that will effect what we have asked. The spaces that seem so silent are full of mighty movement, and this is an immense encouragement to prayer.

And so, for ice-cold hearts we pray,
Who hear and heed not, will not move
To come to Thee, or look Thy way,
Although Thou art all love.

O melt their snow field, Love Divine,
What is there that Thou canst not do?
Thou who hast melted even mine,
Dear Savior, melt theirs too.

Even now, as we pray like that, our Father is moving in ways that we know not, and fires are being kindled that shall thaw their coldness. Prayer in the Name of His Beloved Son cannot lose its way in the void. It must find the ear of God.

For prayer is not emotion, it is a traffic between earth and heaven, "a commerce of love." Our ships set sail for heavenly shores; they do not return empty, it is impossible that they should, but we are not told what tide will bring them back. We think in terms of time: God thinks in terms of eternity. We see the near end of the thread on which are strung our moments, minutes, hours, days, like pearls on a string; the other end is out of view, and yet the thread is one, indivisible. We call the near end *time*, and the far end *eternity*, as though somewhere the thread broke (at death perhaps). But it is not so. We are living in eternity now. God save us, then, from the trivial, the fearful, in prayer as in life. It is an inspiring thing to live in the Presence of the Eternal. It makes it so that we can pile the impossible mountain-high, and still know that nothing can be more certain than this: *The Lord our God and our Redeemer does hear and answer prayer.*

For Love cannot, does not, draw us out in prayer to disappoint us at the last. What man is there of you, whom if his son ask bread, will he give him a stone? Or if he ask a fish, will he give him a serpent? If we have gone far in the ways of prayer we must often have seemed to receive a stone, a serpent—the flint stone of disappointment, or something that stings. "I had fainted unless I had believed to see the goodness of the Lord in the land of the living." We need not faint if we believe to see, and believe to hear too; for deep within us, as surely as Love is Love, a voice will speak, a voice that we know and shall know when all other voices are as the sound of falling waters in the distance. Delays are not explained, but our hearts are reinforced: *"Love will find out the way."* In a richer sense than the old writer meant,

> If the earth it should part him,
> He would gallop it o'er;
> If the seas should o'erthwart him,
> He would swim to the shore;
> Should his Love become a swallow,
> Through the air to stray,
> Love will lend wings to follow,
> And will find out the way.

35

Plowed Under

SOMETIMES an incident that occurs during the writing of a story is like the moth that drifts in with the lighting of the lamp, and settles so quietly that you hardly notice the loveliness that never thrusts itself upon you. For the delicate harmony, fawn and blue, pink and mauve, or the faintest green that ever was thought, the merest whisper of color that makes the pattern on a moth's wing, like the violets by the roadside must be sought out of them that have pleasure therein.

Something like that has come into this room today, for Star and one of our Fellowship, whose Indian name is Premie, have just returned from the taluk of Vishnu's-heaven, where, as the wondering Premie says, they have been walking through the pages of this story from chapter to chapter.

It has been so indeed. To Great-Lake and Red-Goddess, to Uncrowned-King and to the Fort they went together, and everywhere found a welcome. For India is quick to recognize the footprints of the Divine, and the story I have told in part is known to many in that region.

But in the Fort they had their first surprise, for there they found one who knew much of us, and of our children, and, being drawn by what he knew, had, only a few days earlier, set forth on his way to come to see us. He was intercepted. But we see in that thought the flower bud that will open one day. Our Tamil rendering of

Micah 2:13 is "The Remover of hindrances goeth before." There will not always be an intercepting. Who can stand before Him, the Remover of hindrances; whose mighty name is Love?

And now I want to gather the threads of the story of this little lover and tie them, as the Tamils say, into a knot which no hand can untie. ("He ties such a knot with his foot that it cannot be untied by the hand" is their idiom for work that will stand the pull of time and circumstance.) My knot is made of three strands: the way of the Lover of souls with the soul that He calls to Himself, His way as He prepares it to serve unhindered by the flesh, and His way as He answers prayer, working according to a thought of His own that is larger and richer than ours. This third strand is intertwined with the other two from the first page to the last. "I am the Ground of thy beseeching: first it is My will that thou have it; and after, I make thee to will it; and after, I make thee to beseech it, and thou beseechest it. *How should it then be thou shouldst not have thy beseeching?*"

There is little more that I need write about the way of the Beloved with the lover. Love is patient, persistent, wise, tender. Let us work together with Love. And as the Beloved deals courageously with the lover, let us not fear to be brave in our love. God forbid that we should ever fail the soul in its need, but we are not an end to any heart, nor can we ever be. Let us then, not fastening it upon ourselves, lead the child of our love to the Beloved, and laying the dear hands in His, move aside. Of the golden third thread I would only say this: Love will find out the way to fulfil the desires that Love inspires. We have not to do with a baffled Beloved. Who then is willing to pay the price for these eternal gains?

Of all the various figures of the true shown in this story, none more perfectly illustrates the word committed to me than the ancient figure of the plow. "Why should I start at the plow of my Lord, that maketh deep furrows on my soul? I know He is no idle husbandman, He purposeth a crop." Rutherford, whose love to his Lord was no soft emotion, but a passion that did not flinch from the ghastly death dealt out in merciless days to men accused of high treason—he wrote that. Take the words, will to live in the spirit of them, and they lead to the place of singing.

So taken at its deepest, this story is a word of very good cheer. It was written for the most part in a little brown house in the heart of a great forest; and for many days there was rain. Often the trees that all but walk into the house were black in the dark cold air, and the mountains were smothered in cloud and the plains in mist. But every morning, huddled under dripping leaves in the gloom, there were birds that whistled and sang, and the gallant yellow-breasted bulbuls always seemed to be gayest when the grey rods of rain smote the greenwood most sharply. I hope that something of this birdsong has sung through the story. It should, for the way of the Beloved with all His lovers leads straight to the only kind of happiness that is not dependent on fair weather; and He who can make of clay, crystal, and of soft iron, Damascus steel, can enable the least of us for a life, be it a fight in the open or endurance in the shadow, which turns these words to deeds:

Come ill, come well, the cross, the crown,
    The rainbow or the thunder—
I fling my soul and body down
    For God to plow them under.

And this, this only, is the way of joy.

Endnotes

1. Translated from the Catalan of Ramon Lull. E. Allison Peers. SPCK.
2. These early feelings of disillusionment changed, as Star learned to follow her Savior, to a great longing over those who were missing so much because they did not know Him whose Name they bore. And she was used to serve them in later days.
3. *World of Sound*, Sir W. H. Bragg.
4. *The Gospel in the Stars*, Seiss.
5. *The Island of Penguins*, Cherry Kearton.

PUBLICATIONS

Fort Washington, PA 19034

This book is published by CLC Publications, an outreach of CLC Ministries International. The purpose of CLC is to make evangelical Christian literature available to all nations so that people may come to faith and maturity in the Lord Jesus Christ. We hope this book has been life changing and has enriched your walk with God through the work of the Holy Spirit. If you would like to know more about CLC, we invite you to visit our website: www.clcusa.org.

To know more about the remarkable story of the founding of CLC International, we encourage you to read

LEAP OF FAITH

Norman Grubb

Paperback

Size $5^{1}/_{4}$ x 8, Pages 248

ISBN: 978-0-87508-650-7

ISBN (*e-book*): 978-1-61958-055-8

About the Dohnavur Fellowship

The work in Dohnavur still continues, but now the Fellowship members are all of Indian nationality. They do not officially belong to any of the organized churches; but in fellowship with others of God's children, they seek to make His love and salvation known to all whom they can reach.

The dedication of girls to the temples is now illegal, but the Fellowship provides a home for children who might otherwise fall into the hands of people who would exploit them in some way. Girls from five years old to teenagers form a large part of the family in Dohnavur. The need to care for them continues until they are securely launched elsewhere or else have become fellow workers. The aim is still to bring them up to know and love our Lord Jesus and to follow His example as those who desire not to be served but to serve others.

The hospital treats patients from the surrounding countryside. They are from varied religious backgrounds—Hindu, Muslim, Christian. They include rich and poor, highly educated and illiterate. Through this medical work God continues to bring to us the people we long to reach, those whose need is for spiritual as well as physical healing. Boys are no longer admitted, but the buildings they occupied are now put to full use. In 1981 the Fellowship in partnership with other Christians formed Santhosha Educational Society to administer a coeducational English-medium boarding school, primarily for the benefit of the children of missionaries of Indian nationality. The buildings provide facilities for over 600 children now studying there. Their parents come from Indian missions and organizations working in many parts of India, including tribal areas.

In matters of finance, we follow the pattern shown from the beginning of the work. Amy Carmichael rejoiced in her Heavenly Father's faithfulness in supplying each need. We praise Him that His faithfulness is the same today.

The Dohnavur Fellowship
Tirunelveli District
Tamil Nadu 627 102
India

The Dohnavur Fellowship Corporation
36 Templeway
Lydney, Gloucestershire
GL15 5HU
England
ukoffice@friendsofdohnavur.org